PRAISE FOR *THE STORM INSIDE*

"When life feels like a storm, this book will help anchor us to truth while sheltering us with hope. I love the restorative message infused within this book."

—LYSA TERKEURST, *NEW YORK TIMES* BEST-SELLING AUTHOR
AND PRESIDENT OF PROVERBS 31 MINISTRIES

"A warm, comforting, and deeply personal book—reading it is almost like sitting next to Sheila Walsh and having a soul-level conversation about the storms that are hidden in our hearts as women. Her book brought me to tears several times—not because it is a sad book, but because I thought to myself, *Sheila understands.* Sheila gets what it's like to hurt, to struggle, to have unanswered questions, to fail, to lose, and yet ultimately, to trust wholeheartedly in God. It will be a book I return to over and over when my faith falters or I just need to be reminded again of God's unfailing love for me."

—KAY WARREN, SADDLEBACK CHURCH, LAKE FOREST, CALIFORNIA

"Sheila has an amazing ability to communicate the freedom and joy that are yours in Jesus, no matter who you are or what you might have gone through in life. Her passion is contagious and her message is invaluable. I believe this book will transform the way you see Jesus, yourself, and the world around you.

—JUDAH SMITH, LEAD PASTOR OF THE CITY CHURCH, SEATTLE, WASHINGTON

"Sheila gets gritty and honest . . . Shame, unforgiveness, disappointment, bitterness, fear, insecurity, anger, abandonment—Sheila addresses all that and even more in this new book. I highly recommend reading this yourself or buying for a friend. You won't regret it."

—MARK BATTERSON, *NEW YORK TIMES* BEST-SELLING AUTHOR
OF *THE CIRCLE MAKER* AND LEAD PASTOR OF NATIONAL
COMMUNITY CHURCH, WASHINGTON, DC

"I don't say this very often but when I do, I mean it—this book will change your life! Read it as soon as you can."

—CNE CAINE, FOUNDER OF A21

"Sheila Walsh   est truths without sounding superficial or e soul, and lifts the spirit. I am so thankful

—MAX LUCADO

"My friend Sheila knows what it's like to hemorrhage human strength—she *understands* the struggle of suffering and the dark night of the soul. . . . If your world feels like it's spinning out of control, or splitting apart at the seams, this book is for you!"

—JONI EARECKSON TADA, JONI AND FRIENDS
INTERNATIONAL DISABILITY CENTER

"[Sheila's] pen has crafted a beautiful manuscript that has the capability to transform the life of anyone who reads it. You are holding the right book in your hands."

—PRISCILLA SHIRER, AUTHOR AND SPEAKER

"Having faced many of my own storms lately, this book is like an empowering lifeline, reminding me that I am who God says that I am, and that my shame and mistakes do not define me, but instead I am a daughter of the King, with purpose and destiny attached to my life."

—NATALIE GRANT, GRAMMY-NOMINATED, FIVE-
TIME GMA FEMALE VOCALIST OF THE YEAR

"Sheila Walsh has written a book that will encourage, enlighten, and remind us all that through our pains and struggles we are never alone. I really love this book!"

—MAC POWELL, LEAD VOCALIST AND SONGWRITER OF THIRD DAY

"To sit under [Sheila's] ministry is to come nearer to the heart of God. Sheila is the genuine article and I am confident that all who draw near to her story, experience, and wisdom will be forever changed."

—BOBBIE HOUSTON, HILLSONG CHURCH

"For years I've searched for the very best book to offer women who are struggling with a host of painful emotions—fear, anger, shame, bitterness. . . . Here is the hope you are looking for. Here is the truth you need."

—LIZ CURTIS HIGGS, BEST-SELLING AUTHOR OF *BAD
GIRLS OF THE BIBLE* AND *THE GIRL'S STILL GOT IT*

"This is classic Sheila—warm, witty, and winning! Let her help you get beyond the storms inside and find a brighter day in Christ."

—LEE STROBEL, *NEW YORK TIMES* BEST-SELLING AUTHOR

"Sheila tackles topics that could have sent her running from Christ years ago with a candor that is rarely matched . . . *The Storm Inside* is her best work, and it's truly an honor to endorse this spectacular project, as well as the woman who has become a friend, encourager, mentor, and all-around inspiration to me."

—ANGIE SMITH, WOMEN OF FAITH SPEAKER

"I can say unequivocally [Sheila] is one of the bravest women I have ever met . . . so who better to write on hardship and recovery. She has grappled with the unthinkable and has become unmovable in her faith. So allow the counsel of this offering to steady your heart and assure you that you're not alone."

—PATSY CLAIRMONT, AUTHOR OF *TWIRL . . . A FRESH SPIN AT LIFE*

"*The Storm Inside* made me laugh, cry, sigh, and ultimately lean further into the restorative grace of God . . . reading it was like taking a 'trust fall' into His unconditional affection. . . . [T]his is her best book yet!"

—LISA HARPER, AUTHOR, BIBLE TEACHER, AND WOMEN OF FAITH SPEAKER

"Storms can be devastating, but eventually the wind and thunder quiet and the rain moves on. The most dangerous storms we weather are the ones that rage unchecked within. My friend Sheila Walsh opens the book of her life to help you navigate your way to light and hope when your soul is tempest tossed."

—LISA BEVERE, BEST-SELLING AUTHOR OF *GIRLS WITH SWORDS*

"Sheila meets us with the comfort of a treasured friend, willing to ask the questions that lie under the surface of our well-displayed selves and move us to address the feelings that create chaos in our lives. *The Storm Inside* will meet you with love and grace yet compel you with truth and hope."

—JENNI CATRON, AUTHOR OF *CLOUT: DISCOVER AND UNLEASH YOUR GOD-GIVEN INFLUENCE*

"If you are longing to discover the truth of who you really are—read this book. I highly recommend it."

—JACK GRAHAM, PASTOR OF PRESTONWOOD BAPTIST CHURCH, PLANO, TEXAS

"[Sheila] uses her awesome sense of humor and communicates with such transparency about her own challenges that I felt like I could navigate the storms in my own life. Get ready to feel empowered and inspired!"

—HOLLY WAGNER, PASTOR, OASIS CHURCH; AUTHOR AND FOUNDER OF *GODCHICKS*

"Your identity is firmly anchored in Christ's accomplishment, not yours; his strength, not yours; his performance, not yours; his victory, not yours. Which means, you're free! Thank you, Sheila, for reminding me of this. I keep forgetting."

—TULLIAN TCHIVIDJIAN, PASTOR OF CORAL RIDGE PRESBYTERIAN CHURCH AND AUTHOR OF *ONE WAY LOVE: INEXHAUSTIBLE GRACE FOR AN EXHAUSTED WORLD*

ALSO BY SHEILA WALSH

THE STORM INSIDE

Trade the Chaos of How You Feel
for the Truth of Who You Are

SHEILA WALSH

NELSON
BOOKS

An Imprint of Thomas Nelson

Published in Nashville, Tennessee, by Nelson Books, an imprint of Thomas Nelson. Nelson Books and Thomas Nelson are registered trademarks of HarperCollins Christian Publishing, Inc.

Author is represented by the literary agency of Alive Communications, Inc., 7680 Goddard Street, Suite 200, Colorado Springs, CO 80920, www.alivecommunications.com.

Unless otherwise noted, Scripture quotations are taken from *Holy Bible*, New Living Translation. © 1996, 2004, 2007 by Tyndale House Foundation. Used by permission of Tyndale House Publishers Inc., Carol Stream, Illinois 60188. All rights reserved.

Scripture quotations marked ESV are from THE ENGLISH STANDARD VERSION. © 2001 by Crossway Bibles, a division of Good News Publishers.

Scripture quotations marked NIV are from the Holy Bible, New International Version®, NIV®. Copyright © 1973, 1978, 1984, 2011 by Biblica, Inc.™ Used by permission of Zondervan. All rights reserved worldwide. www.zondervan.com.

Scripture quotations marked NKJV are from THE NEW KING JAMES VERSION. © 1982 by Thomas Nelson, Inc. Used by permission. All rights reserved.

Scripture quotations marked MSG are from *The Message* by Eugene H. Peterson. © 1993, 1994, 1995, 1996, 2000. Used by permission of NavPress Publishing Group. All rights reserved.

Scripture quotations marked HCSB are from HOLMAN CHRISTIAN STANDARD BIBLE (HCSB). © 1999, 2000, 2002, 2003 by Holman Bible Publishers, Nashville, Tennessee. All rights reserved.

Thomas Nelson, Inc., titles may be purchased in bulk for educational, business, fund-raising, or sales promotional use. For information, please e-mail SpecialMarkets@ThomasNelson.com.

ISBN: 9780529102683(IE)

Library of Congress Cataloging-in-Publication Data

Walsh, Sheila, 1956-
 The storm inside : trade the chaos of how you feel for the truth of who you are / Sheila Walsh.
     pages cm
 Includes bibliographical references.
 ISBN 978-1-4002-0487-8
1. Suffering--Religious aspects--Christianity. 2. Emotions--Religious aspects--Christianity. 3. Christian women--Religious life. I. Title.
 BV4909.W355 2014
 248.8'6--dc23

2013025856

Printed in the United States of America

14 15 16 17 18 QG 6 5 4 3

This book is dedicated with love and deep gratitude to my friends, Dr. James and Betty Robison. You have weathered some overwhelming storms and have kept your eyes on Christ alone. I thank God for your lives. In loving memory of your daughter, Robin Rochelle Robison Turner, who fought a valiant seven-year battle with cancer. Now home free!

"She will be waiting for us someday at heaven's gates saying, 'Come on, Mom and Dad, and meet the King of kings in all of His glory!' And we will!"
                                                        —James Robison

Contents

INTRODUCTION

Christianity is a battle, not a dream.

—WENDELL PHILLIPS

I spend much of my life traveling. I know airports better than museums and the back stage of an arena better than a park or the ocean. This is my life. I write books and I speak, mostly to women who live around the world, from Los Angeles to New York, from London to Kiev, from Toronto to Sydney.

And I love it!

What I don't love is packing.

My dog, Belle, is deeply offended by my lifestyle. She dreads the moment when I drag my suitcase out of the closet. She understands very well what it means and takes it personally. She walks to the corner of the bedroom and sits with her face to the wall, her back to me—an official shunning. So when an invitation comes that requires no packing or travel, I consider it a gift to the mental health of my entire household.

In the spring of 2012, I received an invitation to speak to a large group of "ministry wives"—the heads of women's ministries and the spouses of pastors and leaders. They gather once a year to receive encouragement from those who understand the strains particular to ministry. For a few precious days they enjoy worshipping together, learning from each other, sharing "war stories," and taking time to receive rather than continuously give. And believe me, directing a women's ministry or being the wife of a pastor or a worship leader has some *very* challenging moments:

"The music was too loud!"
"Why doesn't your husband ever do visitation? Our old pastor did!"
"Bring back the good old hymns!"
"I don't like that translation of the Bible!"
"What happened to the choir?"
"Why does *she* always get the solo?"

It was a beautiful crisp, clear morning, and I stopped for coffee on my drive to the hotel where the event was being held. I think the name of the coffee shop, Global Peace Factory, attracted me as much as the promise of caffeine. I thought of the women I would speak to in just a short while and wondered if Christ's promised gift of peace was tangible to them today or if they were facing such devastating storms that peace felt like a distant dream.

I arrived a few minutes before the morning general session came to a close and slipped into the back of the hotel ballroom. Let me tell you, these ministry leaders knew how to worship! I stood in the dark and drank in the power and truth of words I have loved my whole life:

How great Thou art,
How great Thou art!

The girl responsible for making sure I got to the right place at the right time (a task not for the faint of heart) tapped me on the shoulder, indicating the time had come for us to go. I had about twenty minutes to set up and do a microphone check before the doors officially opened and the women arrived for my session. In front of the podium someone had placed a large cross—which, it turned out, was a gift for me that now sits in my office as an ongoing reminder of what God did in that room that day. The room seated about two hundred, and I touched each seat with a brief prayer for the woman who would sit there and then put a four-by-six-inch card and a pencil on every one. My message would focus on the power of telling the truth, using a simple but potent biblical text:

> Teach me your way, O LORD,
> that I may walk in your truth;
> unite my heart to fear your name. (Psalm 86:11 ESV)

That text holds a special place in my heart, for I've not always found it easy to tell the truth. It's not that I consciously lied . . . I just withheld certain parts of my story. Fear, shame, and anger don't have much curb appeal in the church, and so for years I had stuffed them into the least accessible part of my heart.

That morning I would discover that I had a lot of company.

I am a disciple of Paul in terms of my heart toward ministry. When he wrote his first letter to the church in Thessalonica—a congregation for which he obviously had great affection—he confessed, "We loved you so much that we shared with you not only God's Good News but our own lives, too" (1 Thessalonians 2:8). That is my template. I believe in the power of the Word of God and the transparency of our own journeys.

So that day I told the women that for years I had hidden behind ministry, praying that the work I did for God would somehow tip the scales in my favor and outweigh the feelings of shame and fear that dragged me down. Honestly, I had no idea I could live another way—an unburdened way—based on the finished work of Christ and not on anything I did. It took a crisis in my life to wake me up to that beautiful, radical truth, a crisis of grace that bowled me over like one of those rogue waves that sneak up behind you on the beach.

As I brought my message to an end, I explained why I had placed a card on each seat. I invited the women to write down anything they no longer wanted to carry. I asked them to bring those cards up to the front and leave them at the foot of the cross. I wanted no names—they would remain anonymous—but I promised I would take each card home and pray for each writer.

A beautiful exchange took place that day. I watched as one by one the women left their cards at the cross. Women of all ages, some with tear-streaked faces, laid down their burdens. Our time sped by, and soon they boarded buses to take them to the next event on their schedules. I knelt down and picked up the cards, reading them as I did.

But I wasn't at all prepared for what I saw.

Honestly, the words shocked me.

For the last thirty years I have traveled worldwide, speaking to more than five million women. I have spoken in churches, in prisons, and in arenas filled with women lifting their hands in worship. I have listened to stories of heartache and betrayal, to honest confessions of blatant intentional sin and reckless choices. No matter the age, ethnicity, denominational affiliation or lack of one, the same issues always rise to the surface. Time after time, they fall under the banner of the following ten feelings that can become overwhelming burdens:

- Heartache
- Disappointment
- Fear
- Bitterness
- Unforgiveness
- Anger
- Regret
- Abandonment
- Shame
- Insecurity

So why did I feel such shock that day? The responses on the cards floored me because I knew this room overflowed with women who loved God wholeheartedly and who had walked with Him for many years—*and yet the very same burdens weighed down their hearts*. These women were not new to the faith; they were mature, faithful, and wise servants of Christ—but still, the very same issues stalked them.

I sat with that sobering realization for a long time. I prayed about it and asked God to help me understand why we as women struggle with these persistent and devastating ten issues. It almost seems as though some very intentional, finely tuned plot against us intends to rob us of who we are in Christ. That thought rang true in my spirit like the noise of a thousand bells. I knew God was speaking to me, and I couldn't move on until I grasped hold of what He wanted to show me. I was on holy ground, and I felt it. As I waited on Him, it was as if, for a moment, God in His grace pulled back a curtain and gave me a glimpse of a profound truth that could set His daughters free!

Have you ever read *The Screwtape Letters* by C. S. Lewis? This little book takes the form of a series of imaginary letters from a senior demon, Screwtape, to his nephew, Wormwood, an up-and-coming tormentor. The uncle tries to coach his nephew in securing the damnation of a British man known only as "the Patient." Screwtape gives Wormwood detailed advice on various methods of undermining faith and promoting sin in the Patient. This marvelous book gives a profound glimpse into the ways and wiles of our enemy, often in a tongue-in-cheek fashion.

What if the devil looks over our shoulders on all the confessions we've made to hone an all-out assault on our hearts? It is not beyond his deviousness.

But, girls—what if *The Screwtape Letters* actually provides us with an unsettling picture of the truth? We know from Scripture that Satan is a liar (John 8:44). We know, too, that he prowls around like a roaring lion, seeking someone to devour (1 Peter 5:8). But what if he *tailors* his attacks to fit us, the daughters of the King? What if his demons launch their assaults at the very places where we have shown the most vulnerability? What if he looks over our shoulders on all the negative confessions we've made to hone an all-out assault on our hearts? It is not beyond his deviousness to tune into our pain and turn it into a weapon to use against us.

Even as we speak out about our fear and insecurity, do we give vital information to our enemy? Satan is not omniscient. He is a created, fallen angel and does not know all things, as God does. Through the centuries have we spoken about our brokenness to such an extent that the enemy now has weapons so expertly trained that they can hit their targets, time after time? Have these become "smart weapons," like laser-guided missiles striking from a silent drone? The thought chills me but also reminds me of a much more potent and contrary truth:

> By this you know the Spirit of God: every spirit that confesses that Jesus
> Christ has come in the flesh is from God, and every spirit that does not
> confess Jesus is not from God. This is the spirit of the antichrist, which
> you heard was coming and now is in the world already. Little children,
> you are from God and have overcome them, for he who is in you is greater
> than he who is in the world. (1 John 4:2–4 ESV)

He who lives in us is *greater*! Sometimes we forget that we do not fight against flesh and blood, but against principalities and evil powers (Ephesians 6:12). We desperately need to remember whose we are and how to fight.

A rabbit, it has been said, can outrun a lion. But the rabbit's great fear of the lion *paralyzes* it, making it easy for the lion to catch and consume it. The all-out attacks we face as God's daughters have the potential to render us as impotent as the rabbit. We can be frozen by the chaos we feel inside instead of choosing to stand on the truth of who God's Word says we are. We must not give our enemy such advantages. We must not live that way one moment longer. It's time to trade what we feel for the powerful truth of who we are. How we feel can change in a moment, but who we are is eternal.

There are three levels of reality, of truth, that you and I face each day, and understanding each one of those will be a game-changer for us. There is the chaos of what we feel and the chaos that the enemy would stir up in us. If we focus on those two alone, we are going to go under. The third level of truth is that God is always in control. He is the one who speaks to storms and they have to obey. He is the one who brings order from chaos. No matter how out of control your storms may feel right now, make no mistake girls—God is in control!

In this book we will look at each of the ten chaotic feelings that tend to paralyze us. We will learn how to combat the fiery darts of the enemy, how to fight, and how to stand. We live in dark days, but I believe with all my heart that God is raising up an army of women from all around the world who love Him and who are sold out to one thing and one thing alone: Jesus Christ, our Lord and Savior and soon-returning King.

CHAPTER ONE

When a Tsunami
Hits the Heart

From Heartbreak to Strength

It is such a secret place, the land of tears.
—Antoine de Saint-Exupery, *The Little Prince*

The Lord is near to the brokenhearted
and saves the crushed in spirit.
Many are the afflictions of the righteous,
but the Lord delivers him out of them all.
—Psalm 34:18–19 (esv)

I am an unabashed football fanatic.

To my British friends, I'm not speaking here of that great and glorious sport of soccer, but rather of that uniquely American contest that allows huge men with acres of padding to get hit by the equivalent of a gigantic bull on steroids.

I don't mind saying it took me quite some time to figure it out.

American football, with its blizzard of obscure rules, is not an easy sport to understand if you didn't grow up with it. When I lived in Virginia

Beach, Virginia, friends asked me a couple of times to drive up with them to Washington, DC, for some Redskins games—and then they requested that I stay home or stop asking so many questions.

So much of it seemed incomprehensible to me. Why, for example, when one group of men seems to be doing a jolly good job of getting on with the game, do they all have to head for the benches and let another bunch on after something untoward happens? What exactly is a "down," and when do you know you are down and if you're down in the right place? Why do the coaches throw a hankie on the field if they are not happy with a call? I've always thought when you're not happy, that's exactly when you need your hanky!

Everything changed for me, however, when William, my father-in-law, came to live with us. His patient, knowledgeable presence in our home gave me the key, a way through the labyrinth of rules to the magical land that lies just beyond British understanding. Every Monday night William and I would sit side by side and he would talk me through that weekly NFL contest and gamely answer my onslaught of questions.

"What's a first down?

"Why wasn't that a touchdown?"

"Why so much spandex?"

He had endless patience and knowledge, and for the two years he lived with us before his death, he passed along his insights to me. The last big game we watched together was between the St. Louis Rams and the Tennessee Titans in Super Bowl XXXIV—a *huge* game for us. We lived in Nashville at the time, so *our* team, the Titans, had made it to the biggest stage of all, the Holy Grail of American sports! Before the game I did a little research and discovered that the Rams hadn't won a Super Bowl since 1952. That fact alone gave us more than mere confidence . . . it gave us *unbeatable* confidence.

Since then, the game has gone down in sports history as a classic—but not for the reasons I had hoped.

William checked the television in the den to make sure it looked technologically healthy (he also had a backup set going in the kitchen). I prepared the requisite snacks. Then the big moment arrived. We sat glued to the set, mesmerized by every play. At halftime the Rams led 9-0, but we refused to worry. That's less than a touchdown and a field goal!

"Don't worry, Pop," I said. "We're known as a second-half team."

The second half left us breathless. The teams traded scores, but the Titans crept closer. With six seconds left to play and the Rams still leading by a touchdown, the Titans had the ball. Six seconds might not seem like much, but in football, it's time enough for the kind of miracle that every die-hard football fan prays for so fervently. The Titans lined up on the 10-yard line. Steve McNair threw the ball to Kevin Dyson at the 1-yard line. Victory seemed so near I could smell the fireworks . . . until the unthinkable happened. Rams linebacker Mike Jones tackled Dyson and brought him down just short of the goal line. Dyson stretched for it, and I screeched like a monkey, as if that would somehow inch him forward. But to no avail. Jones had wrapped his bulging arms around Dyson like a two-ton boa constrictor.

Rams fans exploded all over the Georgia Dome as William and I sat in silent disbelief. I will never forget the moment or the look on William's face as he turned to me and, with all the angst of a Shakespearean actor, said, "You have just witnessed one of the most heartbreaking moments in history."

I smile now as I remember the drama of our disappointment; and yet I also recognize how often we use that word in our culture to describe vastly different circumstances. We use it for things that have little weight:

- Heartbreaking that your dog ate your favorite shoes
- Heartbreaking that they have discontinued a favorite shade of lipstick
- Heartbreaking that they killed off your favorite character in a long-running television series

Our culture seriously overuses the word *heartbroken*. It's become as common as rain in Seattle or backpedaling from a politician. But the reality is that heartbreak is profound and real and often as unexpected as a storm that blows in with no warning.

We saw that on May 20, 2013, as an F5 tornado tore through Moore, Oklahoma, leaving a trail of death and destruction in its wake. This tornado, more than a mile wide, stayed on the ground for an almost unprecedented thirty-nine minutes. Those thirty-nine minutes changed the lives of so many. Twenty-three people died that day; seven of those were third grade children, and 377 were injured. As dawn broke the following morning, we began to see the pictures of streets wiped off the map, piles of rubble, toys tossed into trees—the only sign that families once lived there

My first response was to drop to my knees and pray, claiming the psalmist David's promise for those whose hearts and lives were devastated: "The LORD is near to the brokenhearted and saves the crushed in spirit" (Psalm 34:18 ESV).

A team of Women of Faith volunteers joined hands with the amazing ministry of Samaritan's Purse (an international relief agency), and we drove to Moore to join the cleanup crews. Even though I had watched extensive coverage of the tragedy on television, nothing prepared me for what we saw that day. It looked as if someone had dropped an atomic bomb. Row after row of homes had been totally destroyed. It was our job to clear the wreckage brick by brick and pray that somehow we would find for the families who once called this pile of rubble "home" those items that can never be replaced.

Elizabeth asked us to help find her mother's jewelry. We joined hands with the father of an army vet searching for his son's medals. (We found two.) Time after time we heard the same word, *unsalvageable*. Mold, asbestos, or mud had made it almost impossible to save anything. It was a heartbreaking picture of utter devastation. At the end of the day, we had the privilege of spending a little time with one of the men who had lost everything. Samaritan's Purse presented him with a Bible that all the volunteers had signed, and we prayed over him. We had come to serve this man and others who had been affected by the storm, but he was the one who gave us a profound gift.

He told us that just a few weeks before the tornado hit he had been at the theme park Six Flags over Texas with some of the third graders in his youth group. On the car ride home, he talked to the boys about their day and the conversation eventually moved to faith in Christ. One of the boys made it very clear to him that the previous week he had placed his trust in Jesus and nothing could shake that. This boy was one of seven third graders who lost their lives in the tornado.

As we formed a circle and prayed, with tears making paths down our dirty faces, we thanked God for the truth that even as the earth was shaken that day in Moore, this boy had gone from the arms of a family who loved him into the arms of a Father who welcomed him home. Then we prayed for the families of those seven children, for the lives they had known were now unrecognizable. The core meaning of *heartbroken* points to unimaginable loss.

INFINITELY MORE THAN A GAME

As I flipped through television channels this morning at breakfast, I stopped on a news story describing a car accident. A young woman was driving home with her baby safely strapped into a car seat in the back when, suddenly, an out-of-control tractor-trailer plowed into the back of the car, killing the child on impact. The headline spoke of the "latest heartbreaking local story."

The tragedy horrified me; the term *heartbreaking* didn't sound nearly strong enough. We have devalued the word *heartbreaking* by throwing it around so casually, using it to describe things that don't even begin to compare. How could we use the word to describe a football game—and then turn around and apply the same term to the devastating loss of a child?

Perhaps you've been there. You have struggled to find words to adequately describe the depth of your own heartbreaking moment.

- *Heartbroken* that your child has wandered away from the faith
- *Heartbroken* that your husband wants a divorce

- *Heartbroken* that doctors have diagnosed your child with a terminal illness

Somehow, that three-syllable word seems appallingly weak—and doesn't even begin to touch the pain. That kind of agony changes the landscape of your heart.

The winter of 2012 saw record amounts of snow blanketing towns along the East Coast. Entire communities were unrecognizable beneath these bitter, frosty blankets, and as one reporter said, "life as usual was *overcome* by nature." *Overcome* is a strong word that fits well into the vocabulary of the heartbroken. It speaks to something being out of control. As women, we find it hard to accept the reality that we are often powerless. We want to make a difference in a hurtful situation, to do something to help, to protect, to soothe. But times come for all of us when we can do nothing. Nothing at all. And at those dark times, sorrow overcomes us and we feel we won't survive.

The Letters on My Desk

I have the letters revealing our pain on my desk and on my computer, each one telling another story of heartbreak.

"My husband has left me and our three children. What do I tell them? They are heartbroken."

"My son is in prison. I did everything I knew to do. I raised him in the church. My heart is breaking."

"My daughter's cancer has returned. She has gone through so much, and just when we thought she was clear, it's back. Why does God allow such heartbreak?"

These are devastating questions. The word *overcome* doesn't seem to scratch the surface of such primal pain, so we dig deeper.

Overwhelming sorrow or grief > deeply afflicted.

Overwhelm: To overspread or crush beneath something violent and
weighty that covers or encompasses the whole.

To immerse and bear down: in a figurative sense; as to be
overwhelmed with cares, afflictions or business. *(Websters)*

If you have ever walked through a personal storm where you find yourself saying, "I'm not going to make it through this one," your spirit will
resonate with these words:

Overwhelmed

Crushed

Violent grief

The grief component in heartache can lead to terrible isolation. I've
read that when a couple loses a child, the suffering often acts more like a
wedge to drive them apart than a glue to hold them together. That tends
to be as true for Christian couples as for those who profess no faith. We all
deal with pain in different ways, but when we
add prayer and hope and faith to the equation, *At times, the church*
seemingly to no avail, we can easily allow our *has no idea how to*
sorrow to drive us into our own solitary corners. *handle deep grief*

One might hope that the place where heart- *and heartbreak.*
ache is understood and honored more than any
other would be within the community of faith. But I have talked to many
women who have voiced a much different experience. Many have arrived at
a more sobering conclusion: at times, the church has no idea how to handle
deep grief and heartbreak.

Not long ago I met a woman who had lost a child in a random accident.
A few months later she told her Bible study group that on some mornings she honestly didn't think she could make it. Someone saw her cue and
declared, "Just remember this verse: 'I can do all things through Christ who
gives me strength!'"

The grieving woman took a risk and voiced her pain, and instead of being heard and given the space and grace to struggle, she was silenced by a verse that clearly she hadn't lived up to. And how could she miss the clear implication that *if you're not strong, then you're not relying on Christ.*

How unutterably sad.

God didn't give us His Word to use like a weapon or some kind of Hallmark card we can pass across the fence and keep some distance. It *is* a weapon, but one designed for use against our enemy, not against our sisters. It is meant for encouragement, not for pat answers in the midst of real pain. Just because something is true doesn't mean you must voice that truth in all circumstances. Shortly before His arrest, Jesus told His grieving disciples, "I have much more to say to you, more than you can now bear" (John 16:12 NIV). His followers really needed to hear certain true things—things that would eventually help them—but hearing them *at that moment* would have crushed their spirits. So Jesus held His peace.

Oh, that we would read and embrace that memo!

When you hurt, is anything worse than having scriptures randomly thrown at you? How can you catch them when you can barely stand?

I've sat for hours thinking of the many stories like this I've heard, wondering, *Why do we do that?*

Why do we try to "contain" those who suffer or attempt to "fix" them?

Do we think suffering is an embarrassment?

Do we feel personally ineffective in our faith if we can't make the pain go away?

Do we think it detracts from the power and goodness of God when one of His daughters limps around wounded?

For whatever reason, heartbreak makes us *most* uncomfortable.

I have talked to women who have miscarried and heard how others have basically told them to "hurry up and get over it." People seem to have a better knack for dealing with acute illness than with chronic conditions. Short shelf life, okay. Ongoing situation, not so much.

Some years ago I met a very sweet lady who has a continuing and critical health situation. She told me that, during the first year, those around her would ask how she was doing and offer to pray for her. But with no end in sight, she lost her prayer support. I don't know if her friends simply grew tired of praying for the same thing, or if they thought her long-term suffering might indicate some long-term sin. I gave the woman my phone number—something I rarely do—and told her that when she needed to vent, to say things that would curl my mother's hair, she should call me. We all need a place where we can give voice to the worst that torments our souls and still be held.

BEARING BURDENS

Scripture speaks very clearly about how believers should respond to overwhelming heartache. Paul wrote the familiar verse, "Bear one another's burdens, and so fulfill the law of Christ" (Galatians 6:2 NKJV). Just three verses later he wrote, "For each will have to bear his own load" (ESV).

At first reading, these verses might seem to contradict each other; but a better understanding of the underlying Greek words clears up the problem. The Greek term translated *burdens* refers to the thing used for carrying a ship's load. In other words, no one should be expected to carry that huge weight alone. The term rendered *load*, on the other hand, speaks of the heavy packages we all have to carry at times—uncomfortable, perhaps, but necessary and manageable. Think of it as the difference between pulling a wheeled overnight bag behind you in an airport and trying to push a grand piano.

Paul tells us that when someone walks through the kind of heartbreak that feels suffocating, crushing, and overwhelming, the body of Christ must move in to help bear the weight. No one should have to try to carry such a burden alone.

While we might struggle to know how to respond to someone's outpouring of heartbreak and grief, the Bible is brutally honest about the reality of human heartbreak—so honest that I wonder whether we secretly wish to perform a lumpectomy on certain portions of Scripture. These passages feel too raw, too violent, too intense in their description of the storm wreaking havoc on a human soul:

> My heart is troubled and restless.
> Days of suffering torment me. I walk in gloom, without sunlight.
> I stand in the public square and cry for help. (Job 30:27–28)

> "O God my rock," I cry,
> "Why have you forgotten me?
> Why must I wander around in grief,
> oppressed by my enemies?"
> Their taunts break my bones.
> They scoff, "Where is this God of yours?" (Psalm 42:9–10)

One of the bleakest and most heart wrenching of the psalms sits right in the middle of the book. Many psalms begin with a cry for help, but nearly all transition to a confident belief that God has heard and has answered. Not Psalm 88. It begins and ends in turmoil.

> O LORD, God of my salvation,
> I cry out to you by day.
> I come to you at night.
> Now hear my prayer;
> listen to my cry.
> For my life is full of troubles,
> and death draws near.
> I am as good as dead,
> like a strong man with no strength left.
> They have left me among the dead,
> and I lie like a corpse in the grave.
> I am forgotten,
> cut off from your care.
> You have thrown me into the lowest pit,

into the darkest depths.
Your anger weighs me down;
with wave after wave you have engulfed me. (vv. 1–7)

If you wait for a lighter mood, you will wait for a long time. This how it ends:

I have been sick and close to death since my youth.
I stand helpless and desperate before your terrors.
Your fierce anger has overwhelmed me.
Your terrors have paralyzed me.
They swirl around me like floodwaters all day long.
They have engulfed me completely.
You have taken away my companions and loved ones.
Darkness is my closest friend. (vv. 15–18)

Now *that* is bleak.

Why would the Lord include such a dark, depressing song in Scripture? (Yes, it *is* a song.)

Because there are certain storms in life that bear witness to its truth.

There are times in all our lives when the heartache seems unending. Haven't you had moments like that? Haven't you known times when you begged God to intervene, knowing He is powerful enough to change anything; but as far as you could see, He didn't change anything? I know I have.

I walked through a tough situation in 2012 with some friends who had been like family to me for years—and then we had a parting of the ways. I don't think anyone was to blame. It was simply one of those difficult seasons where we each had to choose which direction to take and allow others to make their own choices. If all that sounds neat and tidy—it wasn't. When we chose different paths, I found myself grieving for months at the abruptness of the separation.

I had a hard time sleeping at night. I woke up from terrible nightmares.

At times it felt as if my heart were being torn in two. At my annual physical, my doctor expressed concern about my heart rate and sent me to a cardiologist. After batches of tests, the doctor told me that while I had a healthy heart, my heart rate had spiraled out of control.

"Have you lost someone close to you recently?" he asked, oblivious to my story. Even though no one had died, my loss felt like a death. I had no idea grief could have such enormous physical ramifications. I think that's what Gabriel Garcia Marquez meant when he wrote, "Your heart and your stomach and your whole insides felt empty and hollow and aching."[1]

If you have lost someone you love or walked through a divorce, it can feel as though that furiously personal storm destroyed everything that mattered to you, and you wonder how you will survive.

The Deepest Pains of All

As women, we usually find it easier than men to talk about how we feel. But some pains go so deep and feel so personal that no one else can fully understand our heartache. Even the most empathetic of friends or family can only go so far and no further. If you have not visited that particular place, you cannot possibly know the bitterness of that well.

And it's there, in that place of quiet desperation, that the enemy loves to whisper from his festering cauldron of lies.

"God's not listening to you."
"You are all alone!"
"God doesn't love you."
"You're not going to make it through this one!"

Perhaps you're there right now, barely holding on by a thread. I have been there. I know the dank, bitter smell of that place and how hopeless everything seems. But here's the truth—and I know you might find this hard to take in right now—I also know what it feels like to have Christ walk you out of that cave, by the power of His Word and through other women brave enough to tell their stories. I have seen that transformation in countless lives, in women brought to the very edge of themselves, who found strength instead of destruction.

No, it is never a quick path.

But it is a faithful one.

God has promised that whatever you face, you are not alone. He knows your pain. He loves you. And He will bring you through the fire.

FROM HEARTBREAK TO STRENGTH

Let me introduce you to a young woman I met recently who knows what it means to walk from heartbreak to strength. Her name is Erin, and on the night I met her, she was running late.

Most of us had consumed half our entrees when she finally slipped into her seat in the hotel's private dining room. The sight of twelve chatting women arriving for dinner must have compelled a wise hostess to designate a space apart from unsuspecting casual diners. I noticed two things about Erin straight away. She had a cute short haircut and she was obviously very pregnant. I didn't know any of the women at the table; I had come as their guest.

Several weekends a year I fly into a city at the invitation of a local church to teach a one- or two-day Bible study. I love to spend a little time with the women who organized the event before it begins. I like to hear their hearts, what they hope God will do during our time together. I'm sure you already know this, but women in the local church work extremely hard. Most of the time they organize into committees and cover every aspect of the conference to ensure that the meetings will provide as comfortable, fun, rich, and rewarding a time as possible for those who attend. I have learned over the years that most women's committees want to know more about the guest speaker than talk about themselves. I, as a guest teacher, on the other hand, want to get to know the women. So, once Erin placed her order, I put out a question to the whole table: "Would you each tell us something about yourself that perhaps even some of those closest to you don't know?"

I will never forget that evening. It feels as though it all happened last night.

One by one, the women told stories of disappointment, of serious illness and heartache, and of the mercy and grace of God. But it was Erin's story that stayed with me for a long time.

Erin and her husband, Zac, felt excited to discover after a few months of marriage that they were going to have a baby. But Erin had a miscarriage. Anyone who has suffered a miscarriage knows it brings a very particular pain. Barry and I lost a baby when our son, Christian, was about three years old, and it still hurts.

But Erin and Zac felt their joy restored when a few months later they discovered that once more she was pregnant. On July 1, 2008, Erin delivered their daughter, Adellyn. Every mother waits for that moment. After hours of excruciating labor, someone finally places that little one in your arms. Most of us automatically ask, "Is the baby healthy?"

Erin writes about those first few heartbreaking moments in her blog (www.zacanderinharlan.blogspot.com). She gave me permission to share the following excerpt.

> So at 2:57 a.m. our little girl arrived very quietly. As soon as I looked at her, I knew she had Down syndrome. I asked the doctor if she had Down syndrome and his reply was that he hadn't gotten a chance to look at her yet, but initially, she did look to have some of the features of DS. She had the cord wrapped around her neck 3 times, but Zac was able to cut the cord before they whisked her off to start giving her oxygen . . .
>
> So I laid there helpless while they gave oxygen to this new life. I have never been so scared in my life. Finally I heard a little cry and they were able to wrap her up and bring her to me. I was sobbing. I was in shock, I was scared, and I didn't know what to do. My doctor let me know that all of the feelings I was having were completely normal. That I would need time to grieve for the baby we thought we were having.

It was several hours before I got to see her again. They brought an incubator bed into my room to let me know she was having trouble maintaining her temp and she would be in this bed to help regulate her temp, but she never even made it back into my room before the neonatologist and the pediatric cardiologist were in the room talking to Zac and me and my parents about the findings of the Echo and that Addie was now up in the NICU and would be there for what could be 3–4 weeks.

The doctors left and I continued sobbing. My parents and Zac tried to console me. I didn't understand why this was happening to us. I didn't think I could do it.

As I listened to Erin tell her story that night at dinner, I couldn't imagine what it must feel like as a brand-new mom to face such heartache and questions.

Why does she need to be in intensive care for almost a month?
Why is a cardiologist involved?
What will Addie's ongoing health issues be?
What will her future be like?
How will others respond to my child?

Many struggles and surgeries would follow in the days and months ahead, but as Erin told us the rest of her story that night, it took a turn that I didn't see coming, a turn that took Erin from a place of heartache to a place of strength. What began as a chaotic storm that washed away their initial expectations had resolved into what was now a breathtakingly beautiful new landscape.

When we had finished eating and began enjoying a cup of coffee and our last few moments together, Erin asked me a question: "Would you like to see a picture of my two girls?"

"I'd love to," I said, "but I didn't know you had another daughter."

Erin smiled as she handed me her phone, with the picture of her two girls, Addie and Adrianna.

"She was born in Ecuador," Erin explained. "She has Down syndrome too. When I saw her photograph, I knew she was ours."

I smiled as I looked at the picture of these two sisters hugging each other—and I have to admit, a little part of me went *Bam! Take that, Satan! You thought this heartache would destroy Erin, but in God's hands, she is strong!*

That was just a little part of me. Most of me said, *Thank You, Father, that when we trust You with our heartaches, You make us into warriors for Your kingdom.*

Erin did not come to this place easily. I encourage you to read her blog, for it shows that she has walked a long, hard path, with many moments of heartache, frustration, and tears. But it also shows what Erin did with her heartache.

She took it to Christ. On Addie's third birthday Erin wrote, "I've been listening to the song "Stronger" by Mandisa. I love it and I am believing God."

> 'Cause if He started this work in your life
> He will be faithful to complete it.

The greatest defense against the storm of lies that the enemy would use to drain every moment of joy from your life is to surround yourself with the truth of God's Word. Erin does that in a multitude of ways through church, community, worship, and an ongoing honesty with her Father, who understands how hard this life can be. Rather than allow the storm to isolate her from God's love and care, she continues to throw herself at His feet.

That is the key! And believe me, that is the *last* thing the enemy wants us to do. He wants the heartache to drive us away from God. But when a heartbroken daughter of the King offers her pain and suffering to Christ, the enemy suffers a great defeat. Do we feel strong? No, we feel heartbroken. But when we enter into that divine exchange and take our sorrow to Christ, we become strong in His strength.

Is it easy? No. But when did Christ ever say it would be easy? Remember some of His final words to His closest friends: "Here on earth you will have many trials and sorrows. But take heart, because I have overcome the world" (John 16:33).

Not only did Erin and her husband welcome their own little one with Down syndrome, but she opened up her heart and her home to another little girl who had waited for a long time for someone to see her beauty.

What about you? What heartache do you bear alone? When the storm rages inside, where do you take the pain? In Psalms, David once wrote some stake-your-life-on-them words of truth:

> The LORD is near to the brokenhearted
> and saves the crushed in spirit. (Psalm 34:18 ESV)

You are *not* alone. You are not *alone*. No matter how you *feel*, God's Word would never lie. You are not alone!

CLOSE TO THE FLOOR

On one of the darkest nights of my life, when I literally didn't know whether I would live to see another day, I prayed the simplest, most guttural prayer I have ever prayed:

"Jesus!"

That's it. That's all I could get out.

"Jesus!"

I prayed it with tears streaming down my face and sobs racking my body.

"Jesus!"

I wrote in my journal that same night: "I never knew You lived so close to the floor."

I was familiar with the great words of faith we encounter in our hymns, the words that declare the majesty and glory of God. Those words have often been on my lips, but now I was washed up on an unfamiliar beach, spent, broken, and defenseless. It was here I met with Christ, the One who, though strong, chose to be weak so that when you and I find ourselves too shattered to speak, He sings over us.

STANDING THROUGH YOUR STORM

If you find yourself right now in a place where you are heartbroken, I want to remind you that Christ is very close to the broken. Our culture throws broken things away, but our Savior never does. He gently gathers all the pieces, and with His love and in His time, He puts us back together.

Here are a few things that have brought peace in the worst storms of my life.

1. Call on His name. Call on the name of Jesus. The most powerful prayer can be just one word when it is the name of the One at whose feet one day every knee will bow.

2. Offer Him your heartbreak. Speak it out; tell Him the whole truth. Invite Him right into the darkest, most brutal places—and know that you will be held.

> I lie awake thinking of you,
> meditating on you through the night.
> Because you are my helper,
> I sing for joy in the shadow of your wings.
> I cling to you;
> your strong right hand holds me securely.
>
> (PSALM 63:6–8)

3. Copy out a few powerful scriptures that speak to you onto four-by-six-inch cards and keep them with you. These are a few of mine.

The LORD your God is in your midst,
a mighty one who will save;
he will rejoice over you with gladness;
he will quiet you by his love;
he will exult over you with loud singing. (Zephaniah 3:17 ESV)

When the righteous cry for help, the LORD hears
and delivers them out of all their troubles.
The LORD is near to the brokenhearted
and saves the crushed in spirit.
Many are the afflictions of the righteous,
but the LORD delivers him out of them all. (Psalm 34:17–19 ESV)

Father God,

My heart is broken and I am afraid.

The storm is too loud and the waves are too high.

Hide me under the shelter of Your wings, for You alone are my refuge and strength.

I offer this broken heart to you as a living sacrifice of praise to the God who will not allow the storm of grief to overtake me. In You I am strong!

Amen.

CHAPTER TWO

A LONG, DARK WINTER

FROM DISAPPOINTMENT TO HOPE

*Someone has altered the script. My lines have been changed. I
thought I was writing this play.*

—MADELEINE L'ENGLE, *TWO-PART INVENTION:*
THE STORY OF A MARRIAGE

*We can rejoice, too, when we run into problems and trials, for we
know that they help us develop endurance. And endurance develops
strength of character, and character strengthens our confident hope of
salvation. And this hope will not lead to disappointment.*

—ROMANS 5:3–5

After my very first concert in America, I walked off the stage and into
just four words from my manager: "Well, that was disappointing."
His words pierced my heart like flint. I knew they were true; I
just didn't want to hear them. I'm sure he had high hopes for me as I met the
American public, but I had panicked and stage fright took over.

As a young woman of twenty-six, I was Britain's best-known female contemporary Christian artist. I hosted the first contemporary Christian music show on the British Broadcasting Network; my albums rose to the top of the British charts; I sold out my British concerts. The reality was, though, that I was a big fish in a very, very small pond.

Then Sparrow Records signed me to a recording contract and invited me to tour the States; I would open for another Sparrow artist, Christian guitar legend Phil Keaggy. I flew from my home in London, England, to Kansas City to rehearse with Phil's band. I felt both excited and nervous. Our sixty-city tour would begin at one of the largest music festivals in the country. I had never *seen* a crowd of thirty thousand people, never mind singing for them. A large audience in Scotland amounted to a few hundred people, so the size of this crowd put me several zip codes out of my comfort zone.

I also had all sorts of mandates from well-meaning friends back home, all of them bouncing around in my brain. An elder from my church didn't quite approve of my style of music; he looked suspiciously at any song not in the hymnal. And so this older gentleman gave me some advice before I left. "Your music is far too loud, Sheila," he said in his strong Scottish brogue. "No one will have any idea what you're singing, so make sure you say something important and give a wee word of Scripture between every one of your wee songs."

With that comment lobbed on one side of the net, my manager got ready to serve quite another missile: "Don't talk too much, Sheila. Just sing your heart out on every song. I've told people you're the next big thing!"

I carried the pressure of these competing counsels all the way onto the stage. Earlier that day, as I saw the crowds beginning to arrive, I feared I might panic; so I decided to write something down, something deep and meaningful that I could say at some carefully chosen moment between my loud, apparently incomprehensible wee songs, but something that also wouldn't detract from me as "the next big thing"! When I had finished, I read it over and over and felt sure it would indeed meet with my elder's approval—without bothering my manager too much.

It's one thing to watch a huge crowd from the wings and quite another to stand center stage and see everyone staring at you. No one had ever heard of me, I was new, and honestly, they all just wanted to hear Phil Keaggy. The band began to play the introduction to my first song, and some completely irrational yet strangely persuasive voice inside my head barked: *If you sing faster, it'll be over quicker and you'll be less likely to mess up!*

I sang so fast that I finished the first couple of songs about one verse ahead of the band. I'd confused my musicians, but no more than I had myself. So I just waited silently for them to catch up. To make things worse, I am about as white as a woman gets, so I had *no* moves to fill the dead space. I just stood there, motionless as a corpse waiting for the resurrection.

Sensing that I needed *something* to salvage my appearance, I decided to gift the audience with the profound piece of theological truth I had prepared. I pulled the note out of my jeans pocket and placed it on the music stand in front of me. At that moment, a gust of wind appeared out of nowhere, picked up my sheet of paper, blew it offstage, and then literally dumped it into a trash can.

What to do but improvise? A moment of weighty silence settled on the audience before I offered this profound statement:

"Hello, America! I . . . I . . . I love your hair!"

Really? "I love your *hair*"? Where on earth did *that* come from?

To this day, I cringe whenever someone innocently says, "I love your hair!" I wanted so desperately to say something about the overwhelming love of God, about how God had taken this least-likely-to-succeed Scottish girl and given her a brand-new life—but as I focused on one kind face in the crowd, I could manage only a stuttered statement about her tousled mane. *So* disappointing.

As I walked offstage, utterly humiliated, I could see the disappointment in my manager's eyes even before he uttered his four dismal words.

A HARSH REALITY

Disappointment is a harsh word. It speaks of failure, of not measuring up, of frustration. The word sits right down on your soul and utterly deflates it. It can arrive in something as trivial as a hyped-up movie that failed to deliver, or feel as severe as a blow to the heart that sends you reeling.

If you asked me to pick an adjective that might ultimately lead to hope, I would not naturally gravitate to *disappointment*. Disappointment feels like the mortal enemy of hope. Disappointment saps us. It shouts one more *"No!"* in a world far too short of *"Yes!"*

I sat down recently and read over a couple of hundred letters I've received from women in just the past few months. I had responded to them but kept the ones that really tugged at my heart. The word *disappointment* took center stage, time after time.

> "I wish I'd taken care of my mom and been there for her when
> she was so depressed. I'm so disappointed in myself."
> "My greatest struggle is disappointment in myself."
> "The bottom line is this: I'm disappointed in my life."
> "I am bitterly disappointed in my failure as a mother."
> "I am heartbroken and disappointed in what
> it's like to be a pastor's wife."
> "I'm so disappointed that everything I taught my daughter
> about the love of God made no difference to her.
> She is now in jail because of her addiction."
> "I'm deeply disappointed in how unfulfilled I feel in
> my life in spite of being a Christian leader."
> "I'm disappointed with God. I begged Him to
> heal my marriage and He didn't."

Believe me, the word *disappointed* came up in *far* more letters than these few I've quoted. Of all the issues that seem to hound us as women, disappointment appears to debilitate us more than most. It can turn inward at ourselves or out toward another. It can even get turned toward God.

What would you say about your own experience with disappointment? As you look at your life, can you identify areas where you have faced (or are facing) disappointment?

- Disappointment with yourself
- Disappointment with your marriage
- Disappointment with decisions your children have made
- Disappointment with how your life has turned out
- Disappointment with God

We usually find it much easier to voice disappointment with ourselves or with others than to speak of dissatisfaction with our heavenly Father. It's hard to say it out loud: "I'm disappointed with You, God!" It feels wrong, even blasphemous. The critic in the cellar of our soul reminds us that the Christian life is supposed to be one of victory. No one wants to stand up in a prayer meeting and confess that God has let her down. We want to say the *right* thing, the *spiritual* thing, the *religious* thing, the thing that makes others applaud and say amen!

I love the story told by my friend Dr. Henry Cloud. A Sunday school teacher asked her class, "What is gray, has a bushy tail, and eats nuts?"

When no one answered, she repeated her question. "Come on, class," she implored her students. "You know this! What is gray, has a long, bushy tail, and stores nuts for the winter?"

After more silence, finally one brave boy raised his hand. "Well," he said, "I know the answer is 'Jesus,' but it sure sounds like a squirrel to me!"

Although we don't admit it very often, I think we all want to give the *right* answer rather than what we think might really be *true*. But hear me on this: the compulsion to say the "right thing" explains why so many of us have fallen spiritually sick. If such a thought—that God Himself has disappointed you—lurks in the basement of your soul, then open the door and let it out! I'm serious about this. Stop right now and banish that thought from your mind by the power of the risen Christ. The thoughts and emotions we stuff down into the darkness become a playground for the enemy, where his toxic filth breeds best.

> *The compulsion to say the "right thing" explains why so many of us have fallen spiritually sick.*

"He answered *her* prayers; I wonder, why didn't He answer yours?"

"You've made too many mistakes. God has washed His hands of you!"

"Remember that abortion [or that affair]? That's why God's not
  listening!"

"You are one big disappointment to everyone, even to God!"

All these lies, and a million like them, come straight from the lowest
crypt in hell. They hit us in the gut and take our breath away like a piece of
driftwood picked up effortlessly by a wave and slammed down hard on the
shoreline.

The Truth-Hope Connection

You've probably heard the phrase "Tell the truth and shame the devil." I don't
know where the phrase originated, but it speaks great wisdom. Truth matters
to God, and truth leads to hope. Truth is like a lighthouse on a stormy, pitch-
black night that steers us clear of the feelings that would wreck us.

> Show me the right path, O LORD;
> point out the road for me to follow.
> Lead me by your truth and teach me,
> for you are the God who saves me.
> All day long I put my hope in you. (Psalm 25:4–5)

> The LORD is close to all who call on him,
> yes, to all who call on him in truth. (Psalm 145:18)

> "For God is Spirit, so those who worship him must worship
> in spirit and in truth." (John 4:24)

> So stop telling lies. Let us tell our neighbors the truth, for we
> are all parts of the same body. (Ephesians 4:25)

Do we honestly think we will shock God if we tell Him how we really feel? Do we imagine that we do our souls any good by pretending?

Listen, God is big enough, and His love is fierce enough to deal with *anything* we feel or must face. So let's stop right here and acknowledge the truth: life can deeply disappoint us. God's Word doesn't shy away from it, so why should we? In fact, you don't have to travel very far through the first pages of the Bible to encounter disappointment.

Eve faced the disappointment of knowing that her choice to disobey God led to murder within her own family when her eldest son killed the younger in a fit of rage.

Noah alone among his contemporaries continued to walk with God. If the days seem dark to you now, then just imagine what it would feel like to be the only family on your entire *planet* who loved and honored God.

Turn to Job and the disappointment grows intense. Not only did Job lose his family and

> *Truth is like a lighthouse on a stormy, pitch-black night that steers us clear of the feelings that would wreck us.*

all his possessions, he lost his health. I don't know what kind of relationship Job had with his wife before all this happened, but the tragedy that devastated this couple also withered their marriage.

When we turn to the New Testament, we celebrate the arrival of Messiah—but even though God now walked in human shoes, disappointment remained a daily reality. Consider two of Christ's closest friends, Mary and Martha. When they needed Jesus the most, He didn't show. Their brother, Lazarus, lay dying. They had seen with their own eyes what Jesus could do, healing total strangers. Since Jesus counted Lazarus a true friend, surely He would rush to meet his need! Wouldn't He? But He didn't.

So does the story change after the resurrection? No. We get a glimpse of what disappointment looks like in the life of Paul the apostle. When Paul became a passionate follower of Christ, the hardships and disappointments of life became even more intense for him. He suffered multiple shipwrecks, stonings, beatings, and imprisonment. So it bears noting that Paul was the author of the following profound and challenging statement:

> We can rejoice, too, when we run into problems and trials, for we know that they help us develop endurance. And endurance develops strength of character, and character strengthens our confident hope of salvation. And this hope will not lead to disappointment. (Romans 5:3–5)

When Paul wrote this letter to the church in Rome, he was not a new believer in the first flush of faith. No, he had walked with Christ for more than twenty years, facing some of the harshest disappointments one can face. Do you remember that he had set out one morning full of hope to take the gospel of Christ to Philippi and by that evening he was beaten, shackled, and thrown in a prison cell? In one city he was stoned and left for dead. Paul did not chart his course by the feelings that can so easily overwhelm us but by what he had learned is true. While walking through a dark season, if we attempt to navigate our lives by what we feel, we will run aground onto the rocks. We must navigate by what we know is true no matter what we feel.

From Paul's deep well of experience, he wrote to the early church and to you and me giving us this profound picture—disappointment and hope linked in some kind of strange dance. We will need to unpack this, because normally you and I don't respond to problems with great rejoicing. When I read a verse like this one, I often read it through the ears of friends whom I know face some major disappointment.

I think of Linda, whose daughter, Bethany, faces one surgery after another.

I think of Maria, who battles with infertility and faces fresh disappointment month after month.

Can you imagine saying to Maria as she deals with yet another monthly blow, "Come on, Mari. Rejoice. This is going to help build your faith!" To say such a thing to anyone walking through deep disappointment seems insensitive at best and totally out of touch at worst. I think Solomon had it right when he wrote: "Singing cheerful songs to a person with a heavy heart is like taking someone's coat in cold weather or pouring vinegar in a wound" (Proverbs 25:20).

But (and this is a huge *but*), hear my bottom line: I believe every word of Scripture. God speaks nothing but the truth, and His infallible Word cannot lie. So rather than try to make the Word of God fit my emotional state, I am committed to line up my emotions with God's Word. My emotions can change in a moment, but God's Word is rock solid, so I am learning to drag my emotions in line with what is always true, not just what might *feel* true for a moment. And I want to do so with integrity, not pretense. When faced with a fresh disappointment, I can choose to navigate true north between the currents of despair and denial. For me that usually means an out-loud, honest conversation with God.

Lord,
I didn't see this one coming, and honestly, I would never have signed up for it. It feels overwhelming, but You have promised that disappointment taken to the cross will ultimately lead to hope. So I will set my heart in that direction and drag my feelings in line with the Morning Star.

But let's step back for a moment. If the Lord has promised that our trials and disappointments will lead us to a strong, unshakable hope, then I want to understand how that process works. We live in very difficult days, so pretending that we're fine when we're far from it won't work. We need to fight for a *real* faith that will hold us through the fiercest storms.

Paul knew all this. He didn't write from a comfortable armchair, sipping on flavored tea. Paul knew what it felt like to face bitter disappointment and persecution. And yet, he passionately declared that the problems and trials we face help us develop endurance—in God's hands and in the wondrous, mysterious way He brings beauty from ashes. Endurance, in turn, gives birth to strength of character, which then builds within us a confident hope of salvation. Paul wrote his last statement with absolute conviction:

This hope will not lead to disappointment!

A TURN IN THE TIDE

But I have a question for you and me both.

How can this happen?

How do we move from the darkest night of disappointment to the profound hope that Paul describes? Or must we travel a long, gloomy voyage before even a glimmer of hope peeks over the horizon?

We rarely teach Disappointment 101 in church. And to make matters worse, our culture has very little idea how to handle disappointment.

Don't get me wrong; I love America. I am proud to be a citizen. I love the way we support our heroes. I love the way we celebrate our nation. I love the way we throw out endless opportunities for people to excel . . . but I am concerned about a profound danger hiding among all the beauty and opportunity. *We have forgotten to teach people how to live with the reality of disappointment.* This knowledge doesn't come naturally, and when we fail to learn it, we may feel tempted to throw in the towel at the first feelings of difficulty. Or worse, we may lose weeks, months, and sometimes years of our lives trying to recover from something we feared would destroy us until the storm settles and we see that Christ was in control all along, no matter how things appeared or felt.

Although disappointment hurts, pain does not have to become our enemy. What makes pain our enemy or our friend is how we deal with it. As a mom, I have found this distinction more difficult to maintain than I ever anticipated. I want to protect my son from all life's disappointments! And yet, when I try, I do him a great disservice, for disappointment is part of life. When we fail to acknowledge this fact, we tend to view disappointment as a disaster rather than a chance to learn and grow, a pathway to real hope. For this reason, we must learn to recognize disappointment as a turn in the tide and not the end of the journey.

Not all disappointments are as monumental as they seem at first. And sometimes the little disappointments aggravate the most—a splinter rather than a gaping wound. I have had to learn the latter lesson over and over again!

In the spring of 2012, I joined Weight Watchers. I wanted to lose twenty pounds. That might not seem like much to some people, but it dictated what I could and could not wear in my closet. I didn't know whether this program would work as well in my fifties as it had in my forties, but I decided to give it a shot.

The freedom of the program amazed me. Gradually, week by week, I lost weight, and after three months had reached my target. Wonderful! I was thrilled. What a relief to reach my goal weight!

We must learn to recognize disappointment as a turn in the tide and not the end of the journey.

But then I took an international trip to Ethiopia with World Vision. We flew from Dallas to Amsterdam, Holland, on to Nairobi, Kenya, and then from there to Addis Ababa, Ethiopia. Weight Watchers provides many tools for life in the real world, but they all depend on a trick: you actually have to *use* them. In Africa, we had been told not to eat fresh fruit or vegetables, as they might upset our systems, but no one said a word about cake.

Next I flew to London to join Bobbie Houston and Christine Caine at Hillsong Australia's Colour Conference for Women. We went out for afternoon tea; and when your hosts present you with a plate of homemade scones and cream, well, who would be so despicably rude as to refuse?

I'm sure you can guess the rest of the story.

One by one, the pounds came creeping back. I call them "homing pounds," as they never lose sight of where I live. In the back of my mind, I kept thinking about a Christmas special I had to host, simulcast across America and other parts of the world. I kept thinking, *Next week. If I start next week, I'll have a whole month to shrink.*

Suffice it to say, when I watched the simulcast on my home computer, my appearance did not make me happy. My too-hot dressing room and my too-tight white outfit had conspired to turn me into a large, sweaty snow beast.

Disappointing!

Unfortunately, not all disappointment comes in such trivial or easily fixed packages. Reality can be much, much harsher. Perhaps for years you have been living in a season of disappointment. I used to travel through Europe with my band, and the harshest time to visit many northern European countries is in the winter. If you visit Norway, for example, there is only one hour of daylight. The darkness is pressing and relentless. Perhaps that is how you feel. You have prayed and prayed until you have no words left. You watch others around you and see their lives fall into place. Oh sure, they have their own moments of struggle—but nothing like yours.

I think of a woman who has come to hear me speak every year for the past fourteen years. I look for her in the crowd when I visit her city, and later we find a quiet place to catch up. Her unyielding health struggles debilitate her. Sometimes she will shoot me a text on Facebook or Twitter just to say, "Please pray for me. I feel I am losing hope." I gladly pray and offer whatever words of encouragement I can, but I am deeply aware that I can do little to impact the daily disappointments of her life. I struggle with that. I have no verses or heavenly words of insight to offer a quick fix and no potion to take away her pain.

Sometimes I wonder if believers have an even harder time making peace with disappointment than they do with heartache. If you scratch the surface of heartache, does disappointment lie right underneath? Does this poison keep us sick?

I wonder, because as daughters of the King we celebrate an all-powerful and all-loving God—and the twin truths of disappointment and an omnipotent God of love don't tend to sit well together. Let's imagine you have a child who has abandoned his or her faith. Every night you get down on your knees and beg God to bring your child back to Him. You pray day in, day out, week after week, month after month . . . and nothing changes. At first glance, you seem left with the following dilemma:

God is love, but my child has not come home;
therefore God can't be powerful.

or

*God is powerful, but my child did not come
home; therefore God can't be love.*

The question gets further complicated when we add the fact that some who pray receive *exactly* what they request—by FedEx overnight delivery. So what does that say? Does God play favorites? When we compare lives, it seems hard to believe that the God of the universe loves each of us with the same degree of fiery, passionate love. And if we don't believe that He loves all of us equally, then we struggle to trust Him at all. As Herman Melville wrote,

> The reason the mass of men fear God, and at bottom dislike Him, is because they rather distrust His heart, and fancy Him all brain like a watch.[1]

That surely is the challenge of our faith, to hold these two truths as absolutes, despite the apparent contradiction. God *is* all-powerful, and He is pure, undiluted love. But He is *not* like a genie who appears when we rub the magic lamp and grants us three wishes.

If right now you find yourself in a season of profound disappointment, the enemy would have you believe the lie that God is not listening to you and that He doesn't care about you. He would point to your wrenching circumstances and present them as irrefutable evidence.

As daughters of the King, we cannot live like that! We must hold up, like a shelter, the truth of God's Word over our desperate feelings of disappointment, knowing that He cares and He loves more profoundly than we will ever know.

And Yet the Questions Come

Many of the stories in Scripture give flesh to our many questions about disappointment:

Why did You let this happen, God?
Why did they have to suffer so much for so long?
Why didn't You intervene?

These are deeply moving and difficult questions for me, and they haunt one of the stories in Mark's gospel. No doubt you know it well, so perhaps you will indulge me to dig a little deeper than the details we are given and imagine what the life of this woman might have looked like.

———

She felt lonely, desperately lonely. Some days, when she finally rested her head on her pillow at night, she realized she hadn't spoken a word all day. She had almost forgotten what her own voice sounded like. Day turned to night, over and over again, like a relentless wheel. Soft summer breezes gave way to a cooler season, and she watched it all from her window. On days when torrential rain flooded the streets, carrying leaves and branches to the river and cleaning everything in its path, she wished she could get clean so easily.

Sometimes at night, when the moon hid itself and only the stars lit up the sky, she would leave her house and wander familiar streets. She remembered as a child dancing with her friends and kicking up dust in their wake. She would pass the doorways of friends and family, longing to extend her hand and knock on familiar wood, to see the door open and receive a smiling welcome along with a warm hug, and then get ushered to an honored place by the fire. But she kept on walking.

The darkest nights had become her closest friends. She never walked far; her thin bones made long journeys impossible. She knew her limit, how far she could go before she had to turn around and return home to a silent house. Although her knees hurt, their thin bones pressing on even thinner skin, she knelt beside her bed every night before finding refuge under her threadbare covers. And she prayed: "O God of Abraham and Isaac, God of David—have mercy on me now! Let Your favor fall on me, I pray. I am nothing, the lowest of the low; have mercy on me now. I am unclean and only You can make me clean again. Have mercy on me now." She had lost count of the weeks, the months, and the years she had prayed this very same prayer; but every night, she bowed her knees again.

One morning she heard excited chatter pour through her window as a crowd moved through the street below. They talked about a healer. They spoke of miracles, of blind people receiving their sight—things only a man from God could do. They were heading off to find Him.

She yearned to accompany them, to share in their excitement and their hope—but she had no right to join any crowd. The Law made it clear that unless her bleeding stopped for at least seven days, everything and everyone she touched would become as cursed as she. And yet she wondered, *What if this is my only chance?*

For that matter, what did she have to lose? How could her situation become more desolate than it already was? Her money had dried up, and her reflection became more haggard each time she saw her own image in the water. It was now or never.

She took her old cloak and wrapped it around herself, covering most of her tortured face. She followed the crowd, leaving a little distance between herself and them. Finally, they reached the Healer.

If I can just touch the edge of His cloak, just the tassel, she thought, *I will be healed.* She saw her moment and took it. The Healer had turned to follow another man, and for a moment a slight gap opened in the crowd. With every ounce of strength left in her battered body, she reached out and touched the edge of His garment.

Instantly, like dawn bursting on the horizon, the bleeding stopped. There could be no doubt at all. She sensed a profound wholeness throughout her body. She stifled a little cry of joy that rose to her lips, turning to slip swiftly and silently away from the crowd—when suddenly the Healer spoke.

"Who touched Me?"

She panicked. Her heart felt as though it had stopped in her chest. She thought she could slip away unnoticed, but now she would be exposed.

And yet, the Healer didn't point to her; He simply waited. She waited too—frozen, terrified, alone. She had broken the Law and she knew it, but her desperation had driven her to His feet. She could no longer contain all the sorrow and disappointment that had built inside her. She threw herself again at His feet and poured out her pain . . . and He listened! He listened to her whole story, even though her voice grew hoarse from such an unfamiliar outburst. And then He spoke to her. He looked at her and said, "Daughter, your faith has made you well. Go in peace and continue to be well."

Could it be? He had called her "daughter"! No one had called her anything in so many years—but He called her daughter.

Later that night, as she rested her head on her pillow, she thought, *I wanted the bleeding to stop. That's all I thought I needed. I had no idea I needed so much more. I needed to belong. I looked into the face of God . . . and saw Him smiling.*

———

I often pause at the final words Christ spoke to this woman. I can't help but ponder their significance. He told her to go and *be* healed—but she already *was* healed, wasn't she? The moment she touched the edge of Christ's garment, the bleeding had stopped. So what else needed healing?

So much more!

I believe that woman needed healing from all the lies that had played nonstop in her head for more than a decade. I think she needed healing from the shame and the bitter disappointment. I think she needed healing from the self-hatred she must have worn around her shoulders like a heavy coat. When we limit salvation to a single act or commitment we make to Christ, we miss the beauty and depth of the full-orbed salvation He wants to provide.

She wanted to be healed, but Jesus wanted to make her whole. The Greek word for salvation, *sozo*, means "to save and to heal." Christ wants nothing less for each of us. He wants nothing less for *you*. Christ continues to work in our lives—long after we come to faith—as He exposes the broken places where we have lost hope, inviting us to bring *all* of it to Him. This broken woman gave Christ (and us) the beautiful gift of her story: the whole thing, including the pain and her bitter disappointment. And He received her! She went home that day with a well of hope deep inside her. And not just because the bleeding had stopped! No, she returned home with joy, because she told Jesus the whole truth . . . and it was okay.

Have you ever done that?

Have you ever told Him about the things you have pushed deep into the cellar of your soul, hoping you would never have to look at them again?

Have you ever named *out loud* the disappointments of your life?

The enemy loves to torment us in all those places. He loves to drag out our garbage and face us with the stench. But when we bring out the whole truth to Jesus, the power of a secret long kept simply vanishes. And *only* when you tell Jesus the whole truth, pouring out everything that you see as ugly and unredeemable, can you experience the blessing of hearing Him say in the deepest recesses of your heart, *Daughter, your faith has made you well. Go in peace and be healed of your disease.*

> *When we limit salvation to a single act or commitment we make to Christ, we miss the beauty and depth of the full-orbed salvation He wants to provide.*

Jesus longs to own *all* of you. Are you weighed down by disappointment in yourself, in others, or in God? Tell Christ the whole truth. We will never understand this side of heaven the depth of the love of God. But we have a glorious invitation to trade our disappointment for the sure and certain hope we have in Christ.

STILL MORE QUESTIONS

But many tough questions remain. Christ does not gift every woman with an encounter as dramatic as the one recorded in Mark's gospel. So we ask, if God loves us all equally, then why does one mother plead for restoration of her family and nothing changes, but another mother prays with the same intensity, and quickly finds hope and answered prayer? Why does God sometimes intervene when we pray for healing, but other times no healing comes—or, at least, not in a way that makes sense to us?

I have no satisfying answers. I can only point to what the prophet Isaiah wrote about God: "For my thoughts are not your thoughts, neither are your ways my ways, declares the LORD" (Isaiah 55:8 ESV).

But I do think about John the Baptist.

Toward the end of his faithful ministry, John spoke one word of truth too many in the hearing of the authorities and got tossed into prison. The longer he stayed there, rotting in the dark, the more he wondered. Finally, he sent his followers to ask Jesus, "Are you the one who is to come, or should we expect someone else?" (Luke 7:20 NIV). Maybe his question resonates with you. Perhaps you've done what you thought God had called you to do, sacrificing for Christ's mission—and yet you find yourself in some kind of deeply disappointing "prison." The confidence you once had in Jesus (remember John's early message recorded in John 1:29: "Look! The Lamb of God who takes away the sin of the world!") dies in your throat, and you sink into deep discouragement, wondering whether you got it right or even if God got it wrong.

Jesus did not respond to John as I might have expected. He didn't show up at the prison, put a strong arm around His discouraged cousin's shoulder, and let John into the rest of the story: "Don't worry, John. Everything is going to be okay no matter how you feel right now. Of course I'm the Messiah! Just exercise your faith and I'll get you out of this nasty old jail in no time." Instead, He immediately cured a bunch of sick people, exorcised a bunch of demons, healed the lame, gave sight to the blind (something no Old Testament prophet had ever done; God had reserved this as a sign exclusive to the ministry of the Messiah), and preached the gospel. He then turned to John's disciples and said, "Go back to John and tell him what you have seen," and finally added, "God blesses those who do not turn away because of me" (Luke 7:22–23).

Now, why did He say *that*? I think He did so because Jesus had just performed all these wonderful, liberating miracles for *other* people, while faithful John remained in prison. Blessed is the man or woman who, though bombarded by feelings of disappointment, still loves a God he or she doesn't always understand.

And that's the hard reality of life, isn't it? God, in His sovereign grace, heals some while others remain sick. He raises some from the dead while others die. He releases some from prison while others languish for years—or get executed there. Why? I don't know.

But I do know that sometimes we act as though God is obligated to make all our dreams come true and give a happy ending to every earthbound tale. We use verbiage like "God is head over heels in love with you!" so much that we forget we live in a war zone, where live ammunition flies through the air and casualties still happen. And when *we're* one of the casualties, the feelings that flood in cause us to either doubt ourselves and whether we heard God correctly (since if we had, wouldn't we be out of prison?), or we doubt the goodness, love, or even the very existence of God Himself.

I think maybe that's what Jesus intended in His personal word to John: "God blesses those who do not turn away because of me." Jesus apparently hadn't followed the script that John had expected Him to follow—and who doesn't find it easy to give in to feelings of despair when bad things happen that we think have no place in the script?

Disappointment and prison go together very naturally. Jesus did not offer John the special blessing of a "get out of jail" card—although He certainly could have done that, and, in fact, later did exactly that for Peter (see Acts 12). Instead of opening the prison doors for John, He promised a divine blessing for all those who continue to believe in Him *even when He reads from a script very different from the one we have imagined He must use.*

At this very moment, you may feel a lot like John: tired, discouraged, and confused. And even if you're not there now (praise God), sooner or later you probably will be. Jesus gave John and you and me something solid and hopeful and strong—something "blessed"—to keep us going for the rest of our journeys, whatever they might look like.

John did *not* have it wrong. Jesus *was* the Messiah. God *had* reached down in love and grace to rescue His beleaguered people. And when you continue to believe, despite difficult circumstances, then real, true, divine blessing is yours, even if it doesn't arrive on your doorstep tied in a bow with the trappings you'd expected, hoped for, or wanted.

No, we won't know the true, vast extent of that divine blessing until the final judgment. But what taste of it we get here can still give hope, encouragement, and strength to those who watch God do a work *in* us, even if it's not the one we thought we wanted. Is it wrong or foolish, then, to pray with all our hearts for God to spring us from our prisons? No, not all. In His grace and kindness, He could do exactly that, or even more. But that's His business, not ours.

Our business, whatever comes, is to continue to believe and follow Jesus, certain that a divine blessing *is* coming our way. In the middle of the worst storm imaginable, we tie ourselves heart and soul to the mast of the truth of God's promise that disappointment will lead to hope. It's not that we won't hear the screeches of the enemy's lies in the night, but we will refuse to chart our course by them.

A DEEPER TRUTH

So what can we say about the woman who has faced some agonizing struggle for more than twelve years? What hope can we give?

Perhaps that woman is you. The friend I look for in the crowd every year has suffered far longer than a dozen years. You may feel trapped in a crushingly disappointing situation that looks to have little chance of improving. What does God's Word have to say to you, or to someone who finds herself in a situation from which she can expect little relief on this earth?

Perhaps God is calling you and me to a much deeper truth of what it means to relinquish control of our lives, until all we want is Him. For years the woman in Mark's story had been defined by one thing alone: "Look, there goes that lady with an issue of blood." Now she would no longer be defined by an *issue* but by her *identity* as a daughter of God.

In our sickness we long for healing, but the longing we feel goes far deeper than for any physical healing. We don't know how long this woman lived after her healing, but I can guarantee this one fact: there came a day when she breathed her last breath and passed away. Jesus gave Lazarus back to his sisters after he had lain in a tomb for four days, but one day he also died. (Again!)

The true healing we all long for is nothing less than uninterrupted fellowship with God our Father. No one can touch your identity as a child of God. For every *no!* you have received in life, Christ gives you a definitive *yes!*, which was accomplished on the cross. Paul had it right:

> So we do not lose heart. Though our outer self is wasting away, our inner self is being renewed day by day. For this light momentary affliction is preparing for us an eternal weight of glory beyond all comparison. (2 Corinthians 4:16–17 esv)

This sounds to me like the same essential message Jesus delivered to John the Baptist. We have an eternal hope, kept safe for us by Christ, where no liar can ever touch it. That is not a feeling; that is pure, undiluted truth.

STANDING THROUGH YOUR STORM

Perhaps one of the most keenly felt aspects of disappointment is that it is so debilitating. It's not like the fierce storm of heartbreak that sweeps in and decimates the landscape in a matter of moments. No, it's more like a winter's night that just won't end. Perhaps it is two o'clock in the morning right now for you. If so, my dear sister, I want you to remember that no matter what your feelings tell you, the truth remains—you are not alone.

1. Would you take a few moments and write down, as honestly as you can, all the disappointments of your life, no matter how trivial

they may seem? And beside each disappointment would you write, "Hope does not disappoint!"? Keep it as a faith journal and see over time how God has brought the promise of spring from the longest winter.

2. I love what theologian Miroslav Volf wrote: "Though our bodies and souls may become ravished, yet we continue to be God's temple—at times a temple in ruins, but sacred space nonetheless."[2] Would you be willing to offer worship even now in the ruins of what you see because you are the dwelling place of God?

3. Would you ask God for eyes to see, even through your dark night, others who are cast adrift and be a lighthouse of hope, no matter how dim the flame may feel?

Commit this verse to heart.

"We can rejoice, too, when we run into problems and trials, for we know that they help us develop endurance. And endurance develops strength of character, and character strengthens our confident hope of salvation. And this hope will not lead to disappointment." (Romans 5:3–5)

Lord of all the seasons of my soul, I offer my deepest disappointments to You, believing that You alone can bring morning from the darkest night. Amen.

CHAPTER THREE

NAVIGATING TREACHEROUS WATERS

FROM UNFORGIVENESS TO FREEDOM

Everyone says forgiveness is a lovely idea, until
they have something to forgive.

—C. S. LEWIS, *MERE CHRISTIANITY*

Since God chose you to be the holy people he loves, you must clothe
yourselves with tenderhearted mercy, kindness, humility, gentleness,
and patience. Make allowance for each other's faults, and forgive
anyone who offends you. Remember, the Lord forgave you, so you
must forgive others. Above all, clothe yourselves with love, which
binds us all together in perfect harmony.

—COLOSSIANS 3:12–14

D r. Lloyd John Ogilvie tells a funny story about an Episcopal priest who stood at the lectern of his church one Sunday morning and spoke the traditional words, "The Lord be with you." The people were supposed to respond, "And with your spirit," but they said nothing. Dr. Ogilvie continued:

Since the nave and the chancel (the area of a cathedral closest to the altar) were divided by a distance, the priest was totally dependent on the public address system. The congregation had not heard his opening words because two little wires in the microphone were disconnected. Catching the eye of a fellow priest in the chancel, he banged the microphone in his hand. As he did, the two little wires were reconnected and what he said to his fellow priest was broadcast loudly throughout the sanctuary. "There's something wrong with this microphone!" he shouted. And the people, with rote, patterned response said, "And with your spirit."[1]

Funny story, but it made me think about the deepest emotions that might assault our spirits and drag us under deep waters.

As I have thought and prayed through the issues in this book, I have an overwhelming burden in my spirit concerning forgiveness. A deep, spiritual revelation on *this one issue alone* could change our lives.

The enemy will throw many things at us to try and make us fall: discouragement, fear, shame . . . it's a long list. But I think we make the enemy's job easier in regard to forgiveness. When someone wounds or betrays us, let's face it, we don't *want* to forgive. So many internal voices contribute to the lashing winds in this deadly mental battle:

That was wrong!
It's not fair!
How could she?
You've ruined my life!
They're not even sorry!
If I forgive, I'm letting her off the hook.

Of all the letters I've received from women over the last several years, the most sobering have all concerned forgiveness. Countless lives have been ruined or put on hold because of someone's refusal to forgive. Now, let me say here that I do not believe in "cheap, easy forgiveness." One glimpse at the cross of Christ and it becomes clear that purchasing our forgiveness cost

Him *everything*. True forgiveness should *count*. A halfhearted, "Oh, that's okay, just forget about it," or an insincere, "I can't forget, but I do forgive you in Jesus' name," is unbiblical.

So what is true forgiveness?

Unforgiveness = Rebellion

Many people say they refuse to forgive because they don't feel like it, but genuine forgiveness often does not involve emotion at all. More often than not, forgiveness means dragging our will and our feelings to line up with the will of God, as an act of obedience. Refusing to forgive (whether ourselves or another) puts us in direct rebellion against God.

Does that sound a little strong to you? no

I hope so. Unforgiveness has crippled the body of Christ, handing significant territory over to our enemy. Men stand in the pulpit, week after week, harboring bitterness in their hearts and yet wonder where the joy of ministry has gone. Working in full-time ministry is a calling, not a character makeover; only submission to the Holy Spirit can change our stubborn hearts.

> *Refusing to forgive (whether ourselves or another) puts us in direct rebellion against God.*

Rosalind Goforth, in her autobiography, *Climbing*, recounted the unforgiveness she held on to for years as a missionary in China. Robert J. Morgan retells her story:

> There was an internal rage she harbored against someone who had greatly harmed her and her husband, Jonathan. It was a serious injury that the couple would never afterward talk about, but while Jonathan seemed to easily forgive the offender, Rosalind refused to do so.
>
> For more than a year, she would not talk to nor recognize that person who lived near them on their missionary station in China. Four years passed and the matter remained unresolved and, to an extent, forgotten.

One day the Goforths were traveling by train to a religious meeting elsewhere in China. For months, Rosalind had felt a lack of power in her Christian life and ministry, and in her train compartment she bowed her head and cried to God to be filled with the Holy Spirit.

"Unmistakably clear came the Inner Voice, 'Write to (the one toward whom I felt hatred and unforgiveness) and ask forgiveness for the way you have treated him.' My whole soul cried out 'Never!' Again I prayed as before, and again the Inner Voice spoke clearly as before. Again I cried out in my heart, 'Never; never. I will never forgive him!' When for the third time this was repeated, I jumped to my feet and said to myself, 'I'll give it all up, for I'll never, never forgive!'"

One day afterward, Rosalind was reading to the children from *Pilgrim's Progress*. It was the passage in which a man in a cage moans, "I have grieved the Spirit, and He is gone: I have provoked God to anger, and He has left me." Instantly a terrible conviction came upon her, and for two days and nights she felt in terrible despair.

Finally, talking late at night with a fellow missionary, a young widower, she burst into sobs and told him the whole story. "But Mrs. Goforth," he said, "are you willing to write the letter?"

At length she replied, "Yes."

"Then go at once and write it."

Rosalind jumped up, ran into the house, and wrote a few lines of humble apology for her actions, without any reference to his. The joy and peace of her Christian life returned.

"From that time," Rosalind wrote in her autobiography, "I have never dared not to forgive."[2]

Can you relate to the rage and strength of emotion Rosalind expressed? She had carried that bitterness for *years*. When someone has done something so wrong, something that deeply wounds those we love—and he or she appears simply to have gotten away with it—then everything inside us rises up. God made us to react strongly against injustice. And when the offender doesn't even *care*, well, that just adds fuel to the fire!

As a Christian artist, I did a thirty-city tour with a promoter who ran away with all the money at the end. He paid no one—not the band, not the sound and lighting company, nobody. I eventually tracked him down and felt stunned by his complete lack of remorse.

"What are you going to do?" he sneered. "Sue me? Go ahead. I'll just file for bankruptcy and start up again under another name."

Never in my life had I encountered that kind of calloused heart. I ended up selling my own house to pay the band and crew. I didn't want them feeling the ripple effects of the man's sin. The emotional fallout from that situation stayed with me for some time. Ultimately, I made peace with it by relinquishing it to God. Even though it cost me my home, it was only money.

I thought that I had let it all go until one day a few years later at an artist retreat I saw this man walk toward me. I was not prepared for the waves of emotion that rolled over my heart: anger, bitterness, a festering well of unforgiveness. Standing in the sunlight of a beautiful morning in Colorado I was being battered by the chaos I felt inside. Honestly, I was shocked. I had no idea that I had held on to so much for so long.

I heard God's voice in my spirit: *You brought the debt to Me, but you didn't bring the debtor.* The promoter hadn't noticed me until that moment. When he saw who it was standing just a few yards away from him, he turned and actually ran in the opposite direction. I fell to my knees on the path, with tears rolling down my face as I brought this troubled man to the cross. I forgave him that day. I forgave him with my whole heart. As I knelt and prayed, I was aware of a stone that was beginning to cut into my right knee. I picked the stone up and put it in my pocket. I have it in my office today, a reminder of "Let she who is without sin cast the first stone." I looked for this man for the rest of my time there and never saw him again, but the work God did in my troubled spirit that day changed me forever.

That situation, though troubling, doesn't hold a candle to being betrayed by someone we loved and trusted. Deep relational wounds and soul treachery present a much harder challenge, because they often leave us feeling emotionally ravished.

"My husband left me after twenty-six years to run off with a girl who
   is our son's age. How could he do that?"

"After twelve years and two children, my husband told me he is gay.
   He's an elder in our church. How can I ever face anyone again?"

"My father sexually abused me from the age of ten until I was fifteen.
   How am I supposed to forgive that?"

I have paired unforgiveness with freedom because the two remain
inseparably linked in our spiritual lives. If we will not forgive, then we
cannot live free. We might *seem* free to others, but
internally we remain caged by whatever we refuse to
relinquish to Christ.

*If we will not
forgive, then we
cannot live free.*

This issue has come up repeatedly in raising our
son. Kids hurt other kids without feeling the slightest
bit sorry. My son has stumbled over that ugly reality many times. He would
often cry, "But it's not fair!"

And I would always respond, "I know, darling, it's not fair. Fair doesn't
live here anymore, but Jesus does."

You may not like how that sounds any more than my son, Christian, did
at age ten. Frankly, it didn't impress me either, whether at age ten, twenty,
thirty, or forty. As I've moved into my fifties, however, I have begun to realize the great gift tucked into what sounds like a trite phrase: *forgiveness is
God's gift to us to live in a world that's not fair*.

Some things we can't change. People will cheat, lie, abuse, and just walk
away. But Christ will never walk away. He knows the overwhelming burdens
you carry and offers you a beautiful exchange:

Are you tired? Worn out? Burned out on religion? Come to me. Get away
with me and you'll recover your life. I'll show you how to take a real rest.
Walk with me and work with me—watch how I do it. Learn the unforced
rhythms of grace. I won't lay anything heavy or ill-fitting on you. Keep
company with me and you'll learn to live freely and lightly. (Matthew
11:28–30 MSG)

"You'll *learn* to live freely and lightly," Jesus says. It's a journey, a process, a slow reformation of the heart. The cross has given us a place to take the worst that has been done to us and leave it there for God to handle. But we will do so only if we trust Him and if we believe in His sovereign control, not just with our lips, but also with our lives.

The Cross and Forgiveness

Because I can feel the tension in my own heart, let me say that I know I'm in danger of losing you, especially if your wounds are fresh and raw. Please, stay with me. You may have walked through some outrageous, unforgivable situation. Perhaps you have endured abuse and betrayal at an unthinkable level that would leave us stunned and angry. I do not minimize any of it; I hold all of it to be true.

I hold it all in one hand . . . and the cross of Christ in the other.

Since God has instructed us to forgive, it must be possible. I didn't say easy! He would not, however, command us to do what cannot be done.

The Word of God does not gloss over pain. Far from it! Within the pages of the Bible we find a litany of the most obscene sins committed on the face of this earth, and yet standing above them all is the cross of Christ. Without that, there would be no forgiveness and no mandate to forgive.

"I tell you, you can pray for anything, and if you believe that you've received it, it will be yours. But when you are praying, first forgive anyone you are holding a grudge against, so that your Father in heaven will forgive your sins, too." (Mark 11:24–25)

Get rid of all bitterness, rage, anger, harsh words, and slander, as well as all types of evil behavior. Instead, be kind to each other, tenderhearted, forgiving one another, just as God through Christ has forgiven you. (Ephesians 4:31–32)

> Then Peter came to him and asked, "Lord, how often should I forgive someone who sins against me? Seven times?" "No, not seven times," Jesus replied, "but seventy times seven!" (Matthew 18:21–22)

The number seven often has a highly significant meaning in Scripture. In Hebrew, the number seven is *shevah*, which comes from the root *savah*, which means "to be full, to be satisfied." The number seven often, therefore, speaks of a complete work (but not always). In this passage Christ is telling Peter, "Down here, the need to forgive never ends. You must forgive again and again and again."

WHAT FORGIVENESS ISN'T

Perhaps we should pause for a moment to look at what forgiveness does *not* mean.

- Forgiveness does *not* say that what the person did was okay; people do many things that are far from okay.
- Forgiveness does *not* mean that you have to continue in a hurtful relationship with someone who has harmed and will continue to harm you.
- Forgiveness is *not* burying your head in the sand and pretending the offense never happened.
- Forgiveness is *not* denying the pain.
- Forgiveness does *not* mean we don't take the wrong seriously.

While God calls us to forgive those who have wronged us, some sins still call for civil punishment. A child abuser, for example, must be reported to the authorities.

A young woman once asked me if she had done the wrong thing by reporting a rapist. "You said we should forgive," she said, "but I turned him in." I told her she'd done the absolutely right and brave thing. This man might have gone on to rape other young women. Paul tells us, "The authorities are God's servants. . . . They have the power to punish you" (Romans 13:4). He had in mind the civil authorities, who in his day were the Romans.

Forgiveness is not about removing someone else's liability, but about setting our own hearts free.

Forgiveness is not about removing someone else's liability, but about setting our own hearts free. Did you hear that? It's not about the other person's sin; it's about your freedom. Satan would love to keep each of us in a prison of unforgiveness, bound forever to the one who sinned against us. The enemy has many finely honed darts aimed at the hearts of all who love God—but hear this: he has nothing in his arsenal to combat forgiveness!

Let me say that again: *Satan has nothing in his arsenal to combat forgiveness!*

When we choose to drag the weight of unforgiveness to the cross and, by the grace and mercy of God, leave it there, then the enemy is at a loss. Imagine yourself ransacking the basement of your soul, shining a light into every dark corner and exposing every swollen feeling, every desire for revenge, and every justifiable reason to remain bitter. Now see yourself toss each one into a garbage bag, tie it tight, and climb back out of that place into the daylight. Drag that festering waste to the foot of the cross and leave it there. You are free!

Jesus paid for our freedom—completely, totally, and forever. It might be helpful to write down the worst that has been done to you and find a place to burn it. Even as the smoke and ashes ascend, you stand strong, relinquishing your right to get even to Christ.

"Just As . . ."

So what is forgiveness? How do we know when we have God's complete forgiveness and when we ourselves have truly forgiven others?

We find this central instruction in Matthew 6, in the middle of the discourse often called "the Sermon on the Mount." Jesus gives it to us as He teaches about prayer. Now, when Jesus Himself says, "Pray like this," I want to pay attention! Jesus spoke this prayer to teach His disciples how to pray; He designed it as a model prayer appropriate to those who have a vital, ongoing relationship with God the Father.

> Our Father in heaven,
> hallowed be your name,
> your kingdom come,
> your will be done,
> on earth as it is in heaven.
> Give us today our daily bread.
> And forgive us our debts,
> as we also have forgiven our debtors.
> And lead us not into temptation,
> but deliver us from the evil one. (Matthew 6:9–13 NIV)

We often stop there, but Jesus continued His impromptu lecture. He added, "For if you forgive other people when they sin against you, your heavenly Father will also forgive you. But if you do not forgive others their sins, your Father will not forgive your sins" (vv. 14–15 NIV).

I find it interesting that verses 14 and 15 basically reiterate and unpack verse 12 of the Lord's Prayer: "And forgive us our debts, as we also have forgiven our debtors." This is no small suggestion, but a look into what matters deeply to God.

Jesus inseparably connects God's forgiveness of us with our forgiveness of others. In exactly the same way, the apostle Paul instructs us to forgive one another, "just as God through Christ has forgiven you" (Ephesians 4:32).

Just as . . .

And how did God through Christ forgive us? Of what did He forgive us, and of how much?

The New Testament uses five distinct words to refer to "sin."

- *Hamartia* means "missing the target." We all do that. We were going to lose five pounds before summer!
- *Parabasis* means "stepping across a line." We see the line, we feel tempted to step across it, and we take the step.
- *Paraptoma* means "slipping across a line"—not as deliberate as *parabasis*, but more like what might slip out of your mouth if you drop the iron on your foot!
- *Anomia* means "lawless," a total disregard for what is right.
- *Opheilema* means "a failure to pay a debt." This is the word Christ used in Matthew 6.

Christ laid down His life at the cross, not because you and I might miss the target on occasion, or step across a line to see if we'd get caught, or let something slip out, or even because we chose to live lawlessly. No, Christ said He gave His life for us because we owed God a huge debt that we have no ability to pay. Suppose you were a woman with $2 to her name and an IRS agent tracked you down and said, "You owe the government $2 million, and you have to pay it by nightfall or go to jail."

You can't do it.

No one could.

We owe God a debt we simply have no way of repaying. The debt is too huge and our resources too scant. It's one thing to say to someone, "I'm so sorry that I ran into the back of your car"; it's quite another to have absolutely no means of repaying a gargantuan debt. Only Christ could do that for us—and He did. We had no access to heaven, apart from Christ, and yet because of His supreme sacrifice, we get to come and make it our eternal home, through faith in Him and in His shed blood. Across our broken lives God has stamped: DEBT PAID IN FULL.

And it is from *that* place God calls us to forgive wholeheartedly.

So what does our forgiveness of others look like? Again, it is a process.

Start Where You Are

Who do you need to forgive? Start wherever you are and be honest with God about your emotions. Nothing you tell the Father will be a surprise. You might start with a prayer like this: *Father, I believe that You have asked me to forgive, but I don't want to. Help me to do what's right no matter what I feel.*

Don't wait to feel like it, for that day might never come.

Release that person to God's mercy, rather than asking Him to release His vengeance.

Don't talk about it to others. It's not a prayer request when you are exposing someone else.

Begin to pray for God's blessing on the person's life.

If the bitterness returns, lay it down again . . . and again . . . and again. Seventy times seven.

I assure you, this is not a clinical exercise for me, for I am as much in need of the correction of the Holy Spirit as anyone. When I began writing the words you're now reading, I didn't know God had some surgery to do on my own heart.

After I wrote the first few hundred words for this chapter, I took a break to get a pedicure. I took my Bible and a notebook, thinking that as my feet were soaking I could jot down a few things that you might find helpful.

Well, apparently it was me who needed the help that day!

As I read through the Lord's Prayer again, I heard God's Spirit speak to my heart, telling me that I had not yet forgiven two individuals. Their names came to mind immediately. And I objected:

Lord, that was years ago!
I haven't seen either of these people in more than twenty years!
I don't even know where they live.
I wouldn't know how to get in touch with them.
He tried to destroy my life.

Lord, he didn't just hurt me, he lied about me
to people who mattered to me!
Don't you remember that I once faced him with
it, and he wasn't sorry at all?

My feet sat in a basin of water, but I had forgotten how to wash feet. So my hands went to Facebook on my iPhone; I entered a name, and one of those two faces came up—along with a place to send a private message.

God had made His mandate clear: *ask for forgiveness and do not mention anything he has ever done to you.*

Moments later I remembered that a couple of years ago someone had sent me the other person's contact information, just in case I ever wanted to talk to him.

I sent a text message. I asked only for forgiveness.

It has been twenty-one years. I almost never thought about the offense, but every now and then, if one of these names came up in conversation, I would feel my chest tighten. I didn't see it as unforgiveness. I considered it a "righteous wound" that I bore bravely for the sake of Christ. But that wound of mine, however righteous I may have thought it to be, was still infected.

I put my phone down on the armrest so it wouldn't land in a watery grave, but just a few moments later I heard the familiar *ping* of a text message. I picked up my phone and saw it was from the person I hadn't talked to in years. He wrote, "I gladly forgive you, but do you mind reminding me what happened?"

I didn't know what to do next. I couldn't very well write, "Oh, nothing!"

I kept the message brief and asked if he remembered a particular situation.

He wrote back immediately. "I do now. I was such a jerk back then. God has been working on my heart over the years. Please forgive me!"

Forgiving set us both free.

In his book *Total Forgiveness*, Dr. R. T. Kendall said, "One Sunday I unexpectedly saw a person in one of our services who had seriously hurt one of our children. I noticed them before I was scheduled to preach, and I felt as Corrie Ten Boom must have felt when she spotted her prison guard in the audience. In a flash the Lord seemed to say to me, 'You say you want to see a revival in this church? But what if the beginning of a mighty revival hinges on whether or not you totally forgive this person?'"[3]

Over the past few months, I have felt an internal shift in my heart, a deep call to battle, to stand up and live like a daughter of the King, not like a victim of this world. I consider it a wake-up call to live what I say I believe. My Father is in control no matter how things appear, and if I look elsewhere for things to make sense, I quickly get pulled back into the enemy's grimy net of fighting for what I see as right or fair or just.

Forgiveness is a mighty, spiritual issue. It defies human logic because it's not about this earth. And when by God's grace we choose, willfully and intentionally, to forgive, the enemy is defeated one more time.

What Do You Choose?

If we were to dig though the many layers of our carefully bandaged hearts, it might surprise us to see that at the very bottom, closest to the wound, we have placed God Himself on the witness stand. All our fingers point accusingly at Him, for after all, He could have prevented the whole sad affair.

He had the power to stop the rape . . . but He didn't.

He stood by when, as a child, you cried out to Him for help . . . and He did nothing.

He let the shooter walk right into that school and gun down all those innocent children. Why didn't He at least give the assailant a heart attack?

Jesus understands how agonizing questions like these could be deal breakers. After all, He's heard very similar ones for a very long time.

- "Was it because there were no graves in Egypt that you brought us to the desert to die?" (Exodus 14:11 NIV)

- "Get up, GOD! Are you going to sleep all day? Wake up! Don't you care what happens to us?" (Psalm 44:23 MSG)
- "Lord, doesn't it seem unfair to you that my sister just sits here while I do all the work?" (Luke 10:40)
- "Teacher, don't you even care that we're going to drown?" (Mark 4:38)

Our enemy takes every one of these opportunities to whisper his poison and his lies in our burning ears:

"What if you got it all wrong, Moses?"
"What if you banked on the wrong god, Israelites?"
"What if Jesus isn't as wise and loving as you thought, Martha?"
"What if your 'Messiah' couldn't care less whether you live or die, Peter?"

Jesus calls upon us to follow Him even when we don't understand Him. Remember His word to His cousin John, as "the Baptist" sat imprisoned in Herod's musty jail? "Blessed is anyone who does not stumble on account of me," Jesus declared (Luke 7:23 NIV).

Will *you* love a God you don't always understand?
Will you refuse to be offended by what Christ does not do?
Will you forgive—freely, wholly—so that you may be free?

This is a life-impacting moment. Will you lay it all down? Will you choose to drag your heart to the cross and forgive? Whether you "feel like it" or not?

In his excellent book *Forgive to Live*, Dick Tibbits wrote,

The freedom to choose—the power of choice—confronts you every time you are wronged. Will you choose blame? Or will you choose forgiveness? Will you hand over the reins of your life to someone you don't even like, or will you decide to direct the path of your own future?

His last question is a sobering one. "Will you decide to direct the path of your own life?"

What does he mean by that? I believe he means that we get to choose. We can in essence allow the one who has wronged us to keep choosing our path for us because we won't forgive, and therefore we remain bound to him or her. Or we can choose to submit our "rights" to Christ and choose the path He has set before us.

Dr. Tibbits calls the decision to forgive the "key to taking your first step toward freedom."[4] And he insists that "you can choose to remain bound by those who hurt you—your parents, spouse, boss, or some other authority figure—or you can forgive them and thereby free yourself from their domination. Forgiveness frees you to make the ultimate choice in life: Will you choose to be a victim or a victor?"[5]

Even as I typed those last words, something inside me rose up against how pat they sound, how easy to put on a T-shirt or a bumper sticker. Rarely is reality that neat. But I go back to a statement I made at the beginning of this chapter that this one issue, to forgive or refuse to forgive, could change our lives. I believe that. Many of the enemy's darts wound us and leave us bleeding, but this one poisoned arrow can take us out. I don't mean that we would lose our salvation, as that is based on the finished work of Christ on the cross, but we will lose any effectiveness on this earth for the kingdom of God. Few decisions we make in this life will bear the weight of this one, but the liberating news is that we get to choose.

STANDING THROUGH YOUR STORM

I encourage you to take your time here. Don't rush through this storm. Let it sit and rage within you for a while until it has tossed everything there is to deal with on the shore of your soul. Only then can you make the determination to exchange the lie that nothing will ever change for the truth that in Christ, everything, everything is made new.

1. Begin by asking the Holy Spirit to bring to your mind those against whom you still harbor unforgiveness.

2. Write each name down . . . your own name may be on the list, your mother or father, your husband or child, perhaps even God.

3. Begin the daily, obedient discipline of forgiveness. Don't wait until you feel it; just begin.

4. Find a small stone and keep it close.

Lord Jesus Christ,

You cried out, from a place of darkness and despair so deep that I will never know, "Father, forgive them, for they know not what they do." I choose to align my heart with Your heart. I choose to live like Your child. I choose freedom in Your name.

Amen.

CHAPTER FOUR

COVERED BY CHRIST

FROM SHAME TO LOVE

Ah, but let her cover the mark as she will, the pang of it will be always in her heart.
—NATHANIEL HAWTHORNE, *THE SCARLET LETTER*

Then I said, "It's all over! I am doomed, for I am a sinful man. I have filthy lips, and I live among a people with filthy lips. Yet I have seen the King, the LORD of Heaven's Armies." Then one of the seraphim flew to me with a burning coal he had taken from the altar with a pair of tongs. He touched my lips with it and said, "See, this coal has touched your lips. Now your guilt is removed, and your sins are forgiven."
—ISAIAH 6:5–7

I was born in a land of castles—Scotland has more than three thousand of them, the oldest dating back to the eleventh and twelfth centuries. When you stand inside one of these magnificent buildings, you can almost feel the history, hear the voices, and sense the Celtic music seeping out of the ancient stones around you. Disney castles did not come from Scottish molds! The Scots built their castles for war and to defend their people, not for fairy tales and to delight little girls in Cinderella pajamas.

Although some castles rose over the sites of previous church abbeys, in general, medieval Scots built their castles with military purposes in mind, and because of that, you'll find them in some of the most stunningly breathtaking locations imaginable.

Whether perched on the very edge of a cliff with the ocean pounding the rocks far below . . . on an island at the meeting point of three deep lochs (lakes) . . . or on craggy, snow-covered mountainsides . . . wise architects and experienced builders carefully and strategically chose their locations. The fact that so many castles still stand today bears witness to the skill of the Scots who built them.

Not all our castles are in a glorious state today, however. Far from it. Some ruins are little more than craggy skeletons of their former glory. And it was in one of these that as a young girl I installed myself as queen and claimed my own personal throne.

Loch Doon Castle lies just a few miles from where most of my family still lives. In the summertime, we often visited for picnics with friends. We would spread out our blankets and unpack our picnic baskets outside the ruined walls of the ancient fortress, enjoying the glorious scenery and the sun reflecting off the water. Once everyone got settled in, I disappeared (those were more trusting days).

The castle held a secret that no one else seemed to have discovered. As a fairly agile child, I could step into the large stone fireplace of the one remaining tower and then, resting my back on one wall and my feet on the other, I could slowly climb to the top of the chimney and then crawl out onto the highest remaining point on the castle walls. I stood there at the top of my domain, the voices of my family faint in the distance. On a clear day, I could see for miles across the water.

I became a different person up there. Gone was the girl whose father had died in a shameful way that no one ever liked to talk about or the girl with hand-me-down clothes and one pair of good shoes. Up there, I became a Scottish warrior princess who gladly laid down her life for her people. Up there, anything became possible. I would slay dragons, and when something fearsome threatened to storm the castle, I would fell it with one mighty blow.

Then I would hear my sister's voice shouting up from the bottom of the chimney: "Sheila, it's time to go home. If Mum sees you up there, you will be in big trouble!" So I climbed back down and unwillingly reentered a world with far less to commend it, a world where shame in all its wretchedness ruled the land.

LITTLE GIRL LOST

Many little girls dream of being a princess—if not a warrior one, then the golden-tressed girl who rules the land with kindness. The hearts of some young maidens wait for their perfect prince to come along and sweep them away, or they imagine the beautiful gowns and jewels they will wear.

But dreams get interrupted. Like Annie's.

> *Little girl lost.*
> *Thought no one loved her.*
> *Thought no one wanted her.*
> *Ran away from her castle.*
> *She was embraced by the Devil . . .*
> *Became the harlot.*
> *Became the queen of lies, the Jezebel.*
> *That's my life.*[1]

That's how Annie Lobert describes her life in the *I Am Second* campaign. Like many of us, Annie just wanted someone to love her. Raised by an angry father, she saw her worth through his eyes and it left her aching for so much more.

Annie gave herself to a boy in high school who told her he would love her forever. But he had made the same promise to many girls who started off believing they were princesses too. He broke Annie's heart.

After graduation, Annie left home, knowing she would never look back. She had to work three jobs just to try to make it to college. But then, another world began to open up. In the clubs, she saw what money could do. Her best friend accepted a man's invitation to accompany him to Hawaii one night. Later the friend called Annie and told her, "I'm on the beach, nice car, money. Come and join me." Annie took a break from her jobs, flew to Hawaii, and that first night she and her friend sold their bodies to some Japanese tourists.

Annie became a prostitute.

$500 an hour

$1,000 an hour

$10,000 a night

One evening "Prince Charming" walked into the club where Annie was dancing and told her everything she wanted to hear, everything her father never said. He called her smart and beautiful and charming. He told her he was falling in love with her. She believed him.

And so began her nightmare.

The prince became her pimp. He beat her, broke her ribs, took all her money, and sent her out again to make more. Everything she owned became his. Annie finally got away, but as she says, "When you leave a pimp, you leave with nothing."

The mirror now had an ugly, irreparable crack. For the next few years, not only was Annie's heart broken, but her body betrayed her as well.

Cancer.

Chemotherapy.

Painkillers.

Cocaine.

Demonic darkness.

Then one night, after a massive hit of cocaine and at the lowest moment of all, Annie cried out for help.

"Jesus, please save me!"[2]

Perhaps you think you have nothing in common with Annie. Her story seems so extreme, so rough, so sordid; but if you scratch off just a little of the church paint, it might shock you to discover that we actually look a lot alike.

When someone sexually violates a young girl, dreaming stops.

When the handsome prince uses you and moves on to the next conquest, the dress turns back into rags.

When tender words morph into rage, the mirror cracks from side to side and beauty turns haggard.

The heavy overcoat of shame replaces dresses and swords and jewels, and everything that looked bright and beautiful becomes dull, tarnished, broken.

When you read that word—*shame*—what comes to mind? Several words and phrases come to me:

Wrong

Wretched

Condemned

Worthless

Never good enough

Flawed

Failure

Rejected

Dirty

Humiliated

Less than human

A mistake

Shame is one of the enemy's most powerful tools because it makes so much sense to us. At some level, most of us can admit to a dull yet persistent awareness of not measuring up. Shame, then, doesn't seem like much of a stretch. Shame and guilt often arrive together, but while we can deal with guilt and hand it its marching orders, shame refuses to leave. It's as Edward T. Welch describes it: "Shame is life-dominating and stubborn. Once entrenched in your heart and mind, it is a squatter that refuses to leave."[3]

> *Guilt may or may not be a fact, but shame feels like an essence. It's far bigger than what you did . . . it's who you are.*

Shame is far more subtle and penetrating than guilt.

Imagine that someone accused you of a crime you didn't commit, dragging you through the shaming process of being arrested, stripped, fingerprinted, incarcerated, and humiliated. Finally, you get your day in court and hear the words you've longed to hear: "Not guilty!" The judge removes your guilt. Prison officials return your clothes and possessions to you and you walk into the daylight a free woman . . . but the shame lingers.

Guilt may or may not be a *fact*, but shame feels like an *essence*. It's far bigger than what you did . . . it's who you are.

SHAME VERSUS EMBARRASSMENT

> Shame and guilt have clothed me
> Like a suit of cheap perfume
> Impossible to isolate
> But felt in every room
>
> —MY DIARY, 1993

Shame differs greatly from embarrassment. At the moment, my husband has a fairly impressive blemish at the end of his nose. Over the past three days, it has conquered more and more territory. When Barry looked in the mirror this morning, he announced that he felt ready to audition for the part of a certain well-known reindeer.

Sure, it embarrasses him a bit, but he knows it will pass. Embarrassing things pass in time; shame does not. We can tease Barry about his Rudolph impression, and he'll laugh. No one laughs at shame. It is far too terrible.

Remember the women you met when we started this journey together, the women in ministry? When I read through the cards these women left at the foot of the cross that day, I heard over and over again about shame:

- Shame from the feeling that something is wrong with me—I'm damaged goods

- Shame from my childhood, I can't write it down
- Shame from the secret abortion
- Shame about the affair
- Shame about wanting to kill myself
- Shame from alcoholism
- Shame from incest
- Shame about the rape when I was fifteen
- Shame from sexual abuse as a child
- Shame for what I did to cause a miscarriage at seventeen weeks
- Shame from using the morning-after pill
- Shame for unfaithfulness to me and by me

One card said chillingly, "I just know it would be better for everyone if I were not here."

As I read each card, I felt the weight. Do you know what I mean? I felt the weight that each of these women in ministry carried each moment of her life, her own heavy little secret dragging her down like an anchor on the sea floor.

Shame is the great isolator. Shame has a voice, a vocabulary, and its own peculiar stench. It whispers the sneering threat, "Someone will see who you really are."

As a teenager I dreaded the ringing of the phone. At the first ring my heart began to beat faster until someone else took the call. Logically, it made no sense at all. Every time the phone rang, my gut told me I was about to be found out for . . . something. And yet I had never done anything to be found out *for*.

So why did I react that way? Shame. Shame had talked me into believing that at any moment I might be exposed—no matter that I had no significant skeletons to lay bare. My skeleton was my desperate feeling of absolute worthlessness. Shame is a sandstorm that blinds you to the truth. It feels so overwhelming and relentless that you close your eyes and bow your head and let it rage.

Shame can take two approaches. Shame like mine can come from something done *to* us. Even though we didn't do it, we think we must have deserved it somehow, and that becomes our dirty little secret. Shame also can come from something we've done, something that we dread will get found out. A horrible, powerful little secret holds us prisoner.

I received a letter from a woman who gave me permission to share her story. I'll call her Rose.

When I was a child, I experienced extreme abuse at the hands of my brother and parents. My mother couldn't control her anger, my father was a distant man who was emotionally and physically abusive, and my brother was sexually abusive. When I was sixteen, I had developed quite the drinking problem. I spent much of my teenaged years visiting my mother in the mental hospital. By the time I was twenty-two, my mother had died from cancer, I had fallen into a homosexual lifestyle, drugs, alcohol abuse, suicide attempts, and New Age religions.

That's how I figured I'd fix myself. I had given up on God. I was angry with him. Why did I have to go through all that? I questioned everything I read and was taught about God. I was a Sunday school teacher and felt like such a hypocrite . . . privately I was falling under the weight of my own life.

Rose expresses so well what many of us have felt—that we are falling under the weight of our own lives. Every Sunday, as Rose stood before her class with carefully prepared notes, shame's voice internally mocked her.

If these people knew who you really are, they'd run you out of here!
What if someone tells your secret?
What if someone saw you?

When we read the Word of God through shame's eyes, we may recognize the wonderful truth of the good news of God's amazing grace—but we believe it belongs to everyone else, not to us. The enemy works very hard to get me to believe *I'm the only one.* What a monstrous lie! Go back a few paragraphs and reread some of the cries from the hearts of those women in ministry. Remember, these are not new believers but seasoned followers of Jesus whom God loves to use—and yet the enemy continually torments them with shame. That is why I feel so passionate about exposing him in all his malignant ways, so that every daughter of the King will be able to tell the truth out loud and know she is loved and accepted just the way she is. Until the Lord returns or takes me home, this will remain my pursuit, to fight and expose the enemy in his lies and to declare that the Savior deemed it worthy to blot out our shame before His Father.

DESERVE VERSUS WORTHY

Perhaps part of our problem is that we have confused the words *deserve* and *worthy*. Pay attention the next time a commercial break comes on television. The idea of "deserve" gets pushed at us from every direction.

I am launching an attack on the way we use this word. Our culture has degraded the term to appeal to our baser nature, but no matter how compelling it may seem, it has no power to erase shame.

"You *deserve* to look twenty-one again!"

"This is the car you *deserve*."

"Everyone *deserves* to be happy!"

I hear it over and over again, and every time I do, something inside of me winces. For one thing, it's clearly ridiculous. I *don't* deserve to look twenty-one or to walk around with a permanent grin on my face. This I know. Such commercials may seem appealing, but instinctively we know they lie—and yet we wish they were true. They promise the stuff of fairy tales, and a little part of us would love to believe those fables.

The truth is far greater than any fairy tale. If you subscribe to the lie that you deserve to be happy, you have done nothing to counter the lies of the enemy. In a million little ways he will chip away at the fragile glass palace you have built in your mind, dragging up everything you've ever done and dumping it on the welcome mat of your myth. What Christ offers deals with the garbage of our past, our present, and our future. Shame is real, but at the cross Jesus dealt with shame and gave it an eviction notice. When Christ took our place on the cross, He paid our *entire bill*. When we come to Him in faith, He makes us worthy (not deserving). In ourselves, we could never deserve this love, but rather, while we were yet sinners, Christ died for us (see Romans 5:8). Only Jesus can make us worthy.

The enemy hopes that either you have forgotten this truth or never understood it in the first place. So let's start at the moment when shame slithered into our lives. We need to start with the bad news first and face it so we can see the good news in all its wonder.

It Didn't Start Out Like This

Before we look at how everything went so terribly wrong, we should note that we didn't start out like this. The very fact that something deep inside us longs for more—that we feel our shame and long to be released from it—declares that things weren't supposed to be this way. The world did not begin in shame.

Genesis 3 tells the familiar story of our downfall (if you don't know the story, read the third chapter of Genesis, the first book in the Bible).

> So she [Eve] took some of the fruit and ate it. Then she gave some to her husband, who was with her, and he ate it, too. At that moment their eyes were opened, and they suddenly felt shame at their nakedness. So they sewed fig leaves together to cover themselves. When the cool evening breezes were blowing, the man and his wife heard the Lord God walking about in the garden. So they hid from the Lord God among the trees. (Genesis 3:6–8)

Shame made its debut performance in Eden. As soon as Adam and Eve felt shamed and exposed, they tried to cover up. But their fig leaves didn't do the trick. That's how shame operates. No matter what you use to cover up, you still always feel exposed.

Don't you feel this in your own life? I do.

I don't like how I look, so I buy a new outfit. But even though it looks great in the store, something goes missing by the time I bring it home. *Must be the dressing room lights*, I tell myself. *They've tricked me again.*

You finally lose those twenty pounds that have hounded you for ages. Hooray! The reason you felt so bad about yourself has vanished! But . . . you still feel bad. Why *is* that?

She knew that if she could just get married, the new name and identity would leave shame back at the church door . . . but somehow, it followed her home.

No matter how many layers we slather on to cover up our shame, it remains. Call it a soul sickness.

Adam and Eve knew immediately that their sinful actions had brought dire consequences upon them. Not only did they come face-to-face with their ugly sin but, shortly thereafter, they discovered that shame could not live in the garden. The weight of their shame felt heavy enough; but now they also had to leave. How terribly sad! In moments, they went from enjoying each other and reveling in the holy presence of God to becoming exiles, homeless refugees, banished and expelled from paradise.

What a harsh reality! And we continue to see it today in our own Christian communities.

The son of one of my friends got expelled from his school for drinking on a school trip. The episode felt like watching what happened in the garden played out all over again. First he tried to hide; then came exposure, and finally punishment. It broke my heart. It's one thing to have your sin exposed, but to be separated from your community adds shame to the pile.

A pastor has an affair, he denies it, evidence confirms it, and when he finally owns it, the church removes him from his place of leadership and he gets sent "out of the garden."

The legacy of Adam and Eve gets played out over and over, decade after decade, century after brutal century. But don't lose heart! We serve a God of hope.

Our first parents had been exposed and rejected. That's how it felt to them—crouching in the bushes, dreading the sound of God's footsteps that had so recently filled them with joy. To a degree, that's how shame feels to each of us. Rejection is a core part of the vocabulary of shame. Adam and Eve must have felt acute shock. They once belonged; now they were vagabonds. We can hardly imagine such a horrific shift, from identification with God to punishment with Satan. No longer clothed in the transparent beauty of innocence, now they wore rough animal skins—the blood, perhaps, still dripping from the garments so freshly made for them by God.

Yes, they were covered now . . . but far from clean.

And so they lost their all-access pass to Eden. But God had something else in mind.

WE'RE WITH HIM

Christian traveled with me every weekend until he turned eight. Our friend Mary traveled with us to take care of him when I spoke or sang onstage.

One Friday evening Christian and Mary came over to the arena to have dinner with me, but Mary had forgotten their backstage passes. As she tried to convince a security guard to let them in, Christian saw me walking toward the green room and shouted, "I'm with her!"

Adam and Eve could no longer do that. They couldn't return to the gates of Eden and say, "We're with Him!"

What utter desolation and loneliness they must have felt! Shame *always* brings loneliness. Some provision for the couple's folly had been made, though. Tucked into every hair of the outfit God had made for them, hope lay hidden. It whispered, ever so softly . . .

"You can't cover yourself, no matter how hard you try."

"I will cover you . . . hope is on the way."

As Edward Welch wrote,

The one wearing the skins was covered but certainly not attractive. It left only two possibilities. Either we would forever be covered with the skins of dead animals or this was the first step to a better wardrobe.[4]

And so the Word of God shot the first round in heaven's war on shame. I'm sure the serpent missed it. I don't think it would be clear to Adam and Eve as they wandered, blinded by the sandstorm of shame, but we can see it now. As God shed blood to cover their bodies, every drop of blood pointed to the day when the Lamb of God would shed blood to cover our sin.

Until the coming of Christ, the perfect Lamb of God, Old Testament priests stood in God's presence on behalf of the people. Once again, God took the lead in clothing them—but what an upgrade they got in their outfits! Exodus 28 gives a detailed description of the magnificent robes Aaron was to wear into God's presence. On each shoulder he wore an onyx stone with the names of the twelve tribes of Israel inscribed, six on one stone and six on the other, all set in gold filigree. In a very real sense, Aaron took the people in with him to meet with God.

And so, under the Mosaic covenant, we moved from covered and unclean to covered and consecrated; for in the moment Aaron appeared before God's presence, the people were made holy (at least temporarily).

At times the truth of how God would ultimately deal with our shame is veiled in the Old Testament, but there are moments when it's as if God stills the storm long enough for us to get a crystal-clear view of what is coming. One of those moments is when Moses received very clear instructions in regard to the oils and incense to be burned before the Lord. Exodus 30 details the specified compounds. One special compound they were to reserve for the Lord alone.

This holy anointing oil is reserved for me from generation to generation. It must never be used to anoint anyone else, and you must never make any blend like it for yourselves. It is holy, and you must treat it as holy. Anyone who makes a blend like it or anoints someone other than a priest will be cut off from the community. (vv. 31–33)

Can you guess the contents of this holy oil?

Gather fragrant spices—resin droplets, mollusk shell, and galbanum— and mix these fragrant spices *with pure frankincense*, weighed out in equal amounts. (v. 34, emphasis added)

From generation to generation, the Israelites could offer this special oil to God and to no one else—another sign that hope was on the way.

Now fast-forward through the centuries to a little baby boy, born in Bethlehem. Magi from the east had come to visit this child, heralded by a star indicating the birth of a Jewish King. They offered the boy gifts of gold, frankincense, and myrrh. Do you see the beauty here? Each gift spoke to Christ's identity. The gold, fit for a King; myrrh, foreshadowing His death and burial; but the gift of frankincense shouted, "For God only!" This was the Messiah, God with us.

God is here!

God is with us!

We don't need a priest to intercede for us anymore!

Jesus is here to put an end to our shame forever!

Breathe in the sweet, distinctive fragrance of His presence—it is like no other!

For Annie and for Rose and for every woman brave enough to write her shame down on a simple three-by-five card—and for you and for me— Christ came to take on Himself our shame . . . so that we can be free.

THE GREAT SHAMING

No matter what kind of shame you have experienced, it doesn't hold a candle to what Christ faced on the cross. We stumble into shame; Christ walked right into the eye of the storm and took the full force of its hellish blast.

The exchange began with heart-wrenching prayer.

> And going a little farther he fell on his face and prayed, saying, "My Father, if it be possible, let this cup pass from me; nevertheless, not as I will, but as you will." (Matthew 26:39 ESV)

How can we even begin to understand what Christ had to face? Throughout His three years of earthly ministry, the presence of His Father continually sustained Him. Think of the many times He slipped away from the crowd to pray. At times, He spent the whole night alone on the mountain with His Father.

And now, all that was about to change. He needed a special strength to make it through this desperate darkness, for He knew He was about to take the cup of God's wrath and drink it to its dregs. As all the shame and guilt of the world through all its bloody centuries were heaped upon Christ, His Father would turn away from Him.

In those terrible, incomprehensible moments, Christ would find Himself absolutely and utterly *alone*.

So He prayed for strength. Of course He did! And I'm so grateful to Luke, a physician, for including the following verse in his gospel. Only he records it:

> And there appeared to him an angel from heaven, strengthening him. (Luke 22:43 ESV)

Christ walked into the Garden of Gethsemane, struggling with the darkness of the world; and hours later He walked out, His face turned toward the cross and ready to do the will of His Father. He who knew no shame was about to *become* shame—the very definition of shame—for us so that we could know true redemptive love.

> O sacred Head, now wounded, with grief and shame weighed down,
> Now scornfully surrounded with thorns Thy only crown;

How art Thou pale with anguish, with sore abuse and scorn!
How does that visage languish which once was bright as morn!
What Thou, my Lord, hast suffered was all for sinners' gain:
Mine, mine was the transgression, but Thine the deadly pain.
Lo, here I fall, my Savior! 'Tis I deserve Thy place;
Look on me with Thy favor; vouch-safe to me Thy grace.
What language shall I borrow to thank Thee, dearest Friend,
For this Thy dying sorrow, Thy pity without end?
O make me Thine forever! And, should I fainting be,
Lord, let me never, never outlive my love to Thee!

—BERNARD OF CLAIRVAUX

MORNING HAS BROKEN

Annie was on the floor, desperate and dying, with a plaintive prayer on her lips: "Jesus, please save me! I don't know if You're real, but I don't want to die!"

As Annie lay there, a peace came over her that she had never before experienced. Instantly, she knew that God was real. And yet Annie feared to go to church. Would church people accept and love an ex-prostitute?

They did. As she poured herself into God's Word, she began to hear new words spoken over her:

Loved
Redeemed
Chosen
Beautiful
Set-apart
Whole
Healed
Pure

One day as she vacuumed, God spoke to her and directed her to return to that Vegas Strip and tell the girls still in slavery that they were loved. And that is Annie's life today: redeemed, set free, one who had been shamed now bringing the love of Christ to others.[5] I love this woman. I am deeply grateful to call her sister. The paths Annie and I traveled may appear different, but in reality we are two women who were blinded and decimated by shame, but redeemed by Christ!

What about you? I said earlier that if you scratched off a little of the church paint, many of us "good girls" would not look so different from Annie. We may have sought love and acceptance in alternate places, but when we allow our shame to reign over us in the dark, we all still sit in chains, blinded by the lies of the enemy. Shame is a deeply pervasive feeling because it makes sense to us; it's in the DNA of our fallen lives. That's why we have to fight hard here, girls, for this is a fierce storm! We have to intentionally refuse to allow the enemy to drag those filthy garments out of the trash and drape them over our lives again. We are covered by Christ!

> Now I choose to walk away from what I know so well
> I leave behind this seed of shame and all the lies it tells
> I stand redeemed and worthy here because of Christ the Lamb
> I stand a Daughter of the great I Am

STANDING THROUGH YOUR STORM

In *Shame Interrupted*, Edward Welch gives some helpful steps forward, which I will try to flesh out. He gives us seven insightful steps:

1. Put your shame into words.

2. Turn to your rescuer.

3. Know Him.

4. Be associated with Him.

5. Get your feet washed.

6. Persevere—get ready to fight.

7. Turn toward others: love.

1. *Put your shame into words.* Hard, I know! But the enemy rules in the land of shadows, where secrets live. Take that power away from him. Write it all out. If you have a friend or counselor you trust, talk to her.

2. *Turn to your rescuer.* The word *turn* is huge for me this year. Turning can change everything. In my early twenties, I drove to the most southerly tip of England, Land's End. As I stood with my back to the land, at the edge of a cliff I could see only a drop and then ocean. When I turned around, the scene changed and suddenly the whole of England spread out before me. It mattered where I stood! It's the same here. We can stand with our backs to Christ, staring at our shame, or we can turn to the One who loves us.

3. *Know Him.* Spend time with Him. I used to think that the antidote to shame was grace. Not anymore. For me, it's love. The more I understand the love Christ has for me, the less room my life has for shame.

4. *Be associated with Him.* Many times each day my heart loves to cry out, "I'm with Him!" When I feel condemned or rejected, when someone says something to hurt my heart, I let myself feel the pain. But right on its tail, I remember who I'm with. I take time to catch the fragrance of His nearness. I have an all-access pass into the throne of grace and mercy because I come with Jesus.

5. *Get your feet washed.* People had no choice but to wash their feet in Christ's day. Everyone wore sandals and picked up the dust and dirt of the road. In a spiritual sense, that's still true for us today.

Since we live on a fallen planet, just moving through our day-to-day life causes us to pick up a little dirt. Come to Jesus often and get washed clean. Don't let the dirt accumulate.

6. *Persevere—get ready to fight.* First, you'll have to fight yourself. How easy it is to slip back into shame-based ways of thinking! So fight for who you are in Christ. Others who still struggle with shame will try to call you back in, but don't go there. Don't allow them to throw mud at you, for you are a daughter of the King, and that means you are free. Yes, we have a real enemy—but his shaming days are numbered. He is a liar and the father of every lie ever uttered on this earth. Use the Word of God as your secret weapon against him. He can't stand for long when you brandish it in his face. He *has* to flee.

7. *Turn toward others: love.* No one can take away your identity as a royal daughter. Choose love over hatred, life over death. You don't have to hide anymore. When you get tired (and you will!), read the Gospel accounts again and remember what Christ endured so that you can live with your head held high.

I love to meditate on this verse:

He canceled the record of the charges against us and took it away by nailing it to the cross. In this way, he disarmed the spiritual rulers and authorities. He shamed them publicly by his victory over them on the cross. (Colossians 2:14–15)

You are loved, you are beautiful, you are treasured, and you are a daughter of the living God. Say it over and over again until you find yourself smiling because you are starting to realize . . . *it's true!*

Lord Jesus,
Your love is beyond my understanding but I believe it's true. Right now

I offer You my shame, the filthy rags of my past. I choose to step out of this storm of condemnation and into Your peace. Thank You for loving me and for making me worthy,

In Your great name, amen.

CHAPTER FIVE

A SILENT STORM

FROM REGRET TO REST

The Moving Finger writes; and, having writ,
Moves on: nor all thy Piety nor Wit
Shall lure it back to cancel half a Line,
Nor all thy Tears wash out a Word of it.
—OMAR KHAYYAM, *RUBAIYAT OF OMAR KHAYYAM*

"For I know the plans I have for you, declares the LORD, plans for
welfare and not for evil, to give you a future and a hope."
—JEREMIAH 29:11 (ESV)

I'd never thought of my mother as a shark aficionado, but clearly this five-foot-two-inch maternal powerhouse still had a few mysteries up her sleeve.

"It opens Friday," she said with enthusiasm usually reserved for a new release from the Bill Gaither Trio!

She already had a plan in place.

"If you come straight home from school, we can make the five o'clock showing."

She hadn't convinced me. "Mom," I replied, "this movie is about a humongous shark that eats people! We live by the ocean . . . this might not be smart."

"It's just a movie, Sheila," she answered. "But if you don't want to go, that's fine."

"No . . . no, I can do this," I replied with a whimper.

Jaws, Steven Spielberg's 1975 blockbuster, had just opened in London to rave reviews and had begun swimming menacingly up the freeway to Scottish movie theaters everywhere. Rumors ran rampant.

Gruesome, bloodied body parts litter the beach!

Swimmers dragged underwater, never to be seen again!

Screaming, terror, audience members fainting dead away!

I believed it all.

The movie dominated conversations at my high school as well. Whether you had the right to continue living on the planet appeared to depend on whether you intended to see *Jaws* on opening weekend. I tried not to let my trepidation show.

"I will *definitely* be going," I said across the lunch table. "I'm getting in line early so I can get the best seat possible."

I dragged my timid tail home from school on Friday and changed into jeans and a sweater. I considered the possibility of wearing a turtleneck so I could pull it over my head at the end of the trailers, but the thought of any of the loudmouthed boys from school spotting me proved a sufficient deterrent.

An hour before showtime, a large crowd already had gathered outside the theater. I got in line with my mom on one side and my sister, Frances, on the other.

"Are you excited? I'm excited!" Frances said with annoying confidence.

"Well, of course I am," I responded, startling myself with a voice a little louder than usual, albeit with a peculiar wobble. "But if you have night-mares, which is a real possibility, don't blame me."

Frances rolled her eyes.

My heart pounded in my chest. I don't like movies where things jump out at me, particularly if they then proceed to eat me. Add to that the horror of swimming in water right before they eat me, and I am breathing into a brown paper bag.

The ticket line moved too fast. Four teenage boys in front of us occupied their time with lame shark impersonations. Then our turn came. I stepped forward and before my mom or sister could say a word, I blurted out, "Three to *Escape from Witch Mountain*, please."

"What?!" You could hear my sister's disgust a mile away. My impetuous decision annoyed Frances, disappointed my mom, and embarrassed me.

(I also have to admit that it was a staggeringly poor movie. The average age of the only other people in our theater seemed about ten. I immediately regretted my decision.)

I am a coward!

I am a big, fat, wuss of a 'fraidy cat.

And what would I say at school? I feared to add anything to the inevitable conversations among my peers, lest I blow it. "Could you believe it when the shark spat up that one guy and he was still alive?"

My choices seemed clear. I could either see the movie before Monday or change schools.

Every Saturday night my best friend, Andree, and I went to youth group. I met her outside church the following evening and filled her in.

"Andree, we have to go and see *Jaws*. I don't want to, but I have to or I can never hold my head up at Mainholm Academy again."

The movie was *awesome*! I screamed a couple of times and threw a large bucket of popcorn over the guy in front of me, but other than that, it all went very well. I felt proud of myself. I said good-bye to Andree, apologized briefly to the Lord for skipping youth group, and went home.

"Guess what?" I said to my sister, whom I found curled up in her favorite chair by the fire. My mom stood nearby, ironing some clothes. "I just saw *Jaws* and it was *awesome!*"

Suffice to say, my announcement received a somewhat chilly reception.

Small Word, Big Impact

Regret is such a small word. It might describe one's emotion over a decision as trivial as backing out of a movie or as lightweight as choosing to dye one's hair at home.

At times, however, regret can consume your life.

- You regret your choice of college, convinced that life would have turned out far better if you had attended a different school or chosen another major.
- You regret your choice of husband and fantasize about what life might have been like if you had married that good-looking guy who just joined your church.
- You regret your decision to wait until your career became well established before trying to have children.

When a decision carries weighty consequences, regret can spiral out of control and torment your soul. You may often catch yourself lost in a world of endless what-ifs:

What if I'd said yes to flood insurance? It was a relatively small amount. How on earth will we recover from this disaster?

What if I'd offered to drive home? I knew that my husband had downed a couple of glasses of wine. The accident would never have happened. Lives would not be forever changed.

What if I'd refused to have that abortion? I know that's why I can't have children. God is punishing me.

What if I'd said no that first time when he asked me out for coffee? The affair cost me everything! I threw away my life for a man who proved to be nothing.

Regret punishes us with no end or hope in sight. The Bible declares that the kind of "worldly sorrow" that brings "regret" ends in "death"

(2 Corinthians 7:10 NIV). What Paul is saying in this text is that godly regret leads us to a turning, a moving away from sin to repentance, but worldly sorrow is when we feel we have lost the approval of the world around us and will sacrifice anything, including our spiritual lives, to regain favor. Regret is a tornado that can pick us up and drop us at the foot of the cross or on the other side of the world.

Can you identify your own regrets? They may not seem as serious as those listed above, but they can feel as though they are pulling you under. Failure to deal with regret can effectively ruin lives.

I met a woman who uncovered a sleeping giant after she took her first alcoholic beverage. She decided to start drinking after her husband left her. She admitted to me that she's become an alcoholic. The life of this once successful woman has spiraled out of control. She deeply regrets taking that first drink.

Why did I do it? My life was in a big enough mess. Why?

The harsh truth about some of our decisions is that we can't change the outcome. We can't go back to where we were before that moment. We made a choice, and that one decision affected everything else in our life.

It's a door slammed in your face.

It's the lights turned off with you standing alone in the dark.

It's a dead end.

The emotions of regret can feel as churned up and intermingled as if a tornado had swept through your heart.

Anger
Fear
Shame
Guilt
Pain
Longing
Sorrow
Bitterness
Sick at heart

When Barry and I moved to Dallas, Texas, we bought a house in an area that we considered ideal for our son, who was then seven. We had lots of neighbors with young children. Within a few months it became clear to us—as For Sale signs went up all around us—that our neighborhood was not the idyllic spot we had imagined. Teenage drivers from the nearby local high school constantly raced down our street. We put up signs to try and slow them down, but it made no difference. After an incident when two boys racing each other past our house almost knocked Christian off his bike, I told Barry we needed to move. The housing market favored sellers (remember those days?), so we listed our house. Two couples quickly expressed high interest, and at the same time we found a house in the neighborhood where we wanted to move. We knew someone would snap it up quickly and didn't want to lose it. (I'm sure you can see where this is going.)

We put in an offer for the home we wanted, which the sellers accepted. Before the ink had dried on our signatures, however, the bottom fell out of the housing market and—just that quickly—no one wanted our old home. For four years we owned two homes—a financial nightmare.

I can't tell you how many days and nights I beat myself up over that hasty decision. It obviously doesn't rank with the kind of evil choices that destroy marriages or cripple loved ones, but it severely impacted our lives. I regretted that decision for a long time. I prayed and asked God to forgive us for acting in such a financially irresponsible way, and I knew He did; but we still had to live with the consequences.

In *David Copperfield*, my favorite of Charles Dickens's works, we read, "It was a long and gloomy night that gathered on me, haunted by the ghosts of many hopes, of many dear remembrances, many errors, many unavailing sorrows . . ."

That is how regret feels—like a long, gloomy night with no sign of dawn on the horizon. Whether we regret something we have done, something others have done to us, or something we ought to have done but didn't, regret has a way of grabbing the spotlight on the human stage. It tends to fall into four general categories:

- We regret things we have done.
- We regret things we have failed to do.
- We regret things others have done to us.
- We regret things others didn't do.

Other types of regret certainly exist, but they don't tend to consume us with nearly as much ferocity as these four. Our insurance companies, for example, call natural disasters "acts of God." If a tornado rips through town and destroys your home, the tragedy devastates you. But you don't feel the same weight of regret, because what could you have done? You might feel anger, sadness, or even depression, but seldom regret.

Or we might watch our children growing up and feel an ache at how rapidly they seem to be turning into young men and women. But unless we have made some really poor parenting choices, that's not regret so much as the inevitability of life. The other day I found a pair of the first baby shoes we bought for Christian. I sat them beside the two canoes his feet currently require and thought how much I miss those days when he would drag his little dinosaur around the house. A poignant moment? Certainly. But not regret. I just got hit with a heavy dose of nostalgia coupled with a mother's love.

True regret, however, can alter the landscape of our lives and our relationships. Just as the fiercest tornado can eradicate what was once ours, regret can threaten us with the lie that our lives have been irrevocably ruined.

REGRET FOR WHAT WE HAVE DONE

This is a huge issue for us as women. It becomes particularly difficult if we've done something that, in our gut, we recognized as wrong. As Christian women, the guilt can become even more pronounced.

A young woman who had an affair in the first year of her marriage wrote me to say, "How can I ever forgive myself? I knew it was wrong and I did it anyway. I know the scripture that says God will never give us more than we can bear, but will always give us a way of escape. I knew that. I felt that, but I did it anyway. How can there be forgiveness for that?"

Another young woman wrote, "My husband wants to be a dad so badly, but I don't feel ready. So when I got pregnant, I didn't tell him. I had an abortion and I never told him. Even if God would forgive me, my husband never would. I feel as if I am dying inside."

Situations like these practically invite the enemy to torment us.

You call yourself a Christian? You're a hypocrite!
You betrayed those who loved you. What kind of woman are you?
If anyone finds out what you did, it's over for you . . . you'll be ruined!

Have thoughts like that ever tormented you? Do you have regrets for something you've done but see no way out? Let me remind you what God's Word says about our sin.

> "Come now, let us reason together, says the LORD:
> though your sins are like scarlet,
> they shall be as white as snow;
> though they are red like crimson,
> they shall become like wool." (Isaiah 1:18 ESV)

Do you remember what the Romans did to Jesus before He died to pay for our sin?

> Then the soldiers of the governor took Jesus into the governor's headquarters, and they gathered the whole battalion before him. And they stripped him and put a scarlet robe on him. (Matthew 27:27–28 ESV)

Roman soldiers dressed the pure, spotless Lamb of God in scarlet—a symbol of our sin—as He prepared the way for us to be made white as snow. I find this remarkable, that God would orchestrate every imaginable facet of our redemption, even down to the symbolism involved.

We see the color scarlet woven throughout Scripture. You can trace the blood drops in Eden to the doorposts in Egypt painted with the blood of Passover lambs. Then notice that this scarlet thread makes an unexpected stop in Jericho. Do you remember?

The color scarlet changed the life of Rahab, a prostitute. You'll find her dramatic story in Joshua 2.

When the Israelites crossed the Jordan River into Canaan, they encountered a huge problem. The fortified city of Jericho in all its intimidating bulk blocked access to the heart of the promised land. The city's massive fortifications made storming it impossible, and Israel was neither ready nor equipped for a long siege. Not only that, but a prolonged siege would give the Canaanites time to unite and overwhelm them. So Joshua sent two spies to look over the city.

The men needed a place to hide—but where? Of all people, Rahab the prostitute gave them shelter. Scripture tells us they came to her house and "stayed there that night" (Joshua 2:1). Excuse me? They stayed there all night? At a pagan prostitute's house? Just try to get *that* past the church mission board!

Scripture tells a lot of outrageous stories such as this one. But in every such story, if we dig a little deeper, we come face-to-face with the shocking, over-the-top, at times offensive love of God. The stories never highlight the depravity of the people, but rather magnify the greatness and goodness of God. That's Rahab's story exactly.

We don't know why or when she became a prostitute, but when we meet her, she wants to change her life. I find it compelling that Rahab moves from regret to action, and that action leads to rest—not only for Rahab and her family, but also for generations to come. (Rahab is one of only four women mentioned in the genealogy of Christ!)

When the king's guards come to Rahab's door to ask about the spies, we see her at the most important crossroads of her life. If she turns in the men, she'll get a reward. If she shelters them, she has no reason to believe they will do anything for her. Why would they? But Rahab in effect takes a step of faith from a past she regrets into the promise of a future she longs for so she shelters the spies. All she asks is that when the city is destroyed they save her and her family.

The spies gave Rahab just one small but critical instruction: "When we come into the land, you must leave this scarlet rope hanging from the window through which you let us down" (v. 18).

A little while later, when the city walls collapsed and the Israelites stormed into Jericho, only one family survived: Rahab's. They survived because of a scarlet cord hanging from a window. We don't know anything about the lives of Rahab's family or what kind of people they were, because it doesn't matter. What saved them—what saves you and me—was the scarlet cord, the blood over the doorpost: the shed blood of Christ. Hang that scarlet cord from the window of your soul, and don't let regret for what you have done rob you of the joy of who you are!

In his letter to the Colossians, Paul wrote one of my favorite passages that speaks to the finality of Christ dealing with our sin on the cross.

> You were dead because of your sins and because your sinful nature was not yet cut away. Then God made you alive with Christ, for he forgave all our sins. He canceled the record of the charges against us and took it away by nailing it to the cross. In this way, he disarmed the spiritual rulers and authorities. He shamed them publicly by his victory over them on the cross. (Colossians 2:13–15)

Christ canceled our record of sin! We all have a bill we cannot pay. Only Jesus has the resources to forgive this debt.

When Paul wrote that Christ *canceled* our debt, he had a different picture in mind than what normally comes into our heads. Writers in Paul's day wrote either on vellum or papyrus, both expensive materials. The ink used back then contained no acid, and acid is what makes ink instantly lock into paper. One could remove writing from vellum or papyrus (before it dried) simply by wiping the paper. That's the image Paul had in mind. When we confess our sins, Christ wipes our slates clean. Not even the indentation of the words remains!

But although Christ has dealt with our sin, we still have to walk out the consequences of our choices. The young woman who had the affair can own her sin, but she has no control over how her husband will respond. Still, keeping her secret is making her sick. I therefore advised her to find a truly trustworthy counselor to whom she could confess her sin, someone who would love her and share the grace and mercy of God with her and walk with her on this journey.

> Confess your sins to each other and pray for each other so that you may be healed. (James 5:16)

> Godly sorrow brings repentance that leads to salvation and leaves no regret, but worldly sorrow brings death. (2 Corinthians 7:10 NIV)

The peculiar sickness of regret requires prayer. We may feel desperately disappointed to have to face our sinfulness, but Jesus came to enable us to do exactly that.

But He doesn't just leave us there.

He gives us the strength to face our sinfulness so that He can direct us back onto the path of life. And only on that path will we find the rest we seek:

> This is what the LORD says:
> "Stand at the crossroads and look;
> ask for the ancient paths,
> ask where the good way is, and walk in it,
>   and you will find rest for your souls." (Jeremiah 6:16 NIV)

Regret for What We Didn't Do

One of the saddest stories I ever watched on the news told of a fatal fire that began when a woman left something on the stove. She managed to get two of

her children out, but her youngest died in the flames. I found myself sobbing
with her as she cried out, "Why didn't I check the stove?" It felt excruciating
to watch her pain. Not only had she lost a child but she also blamed herself.

Overwhelming regret!

The *Harvard Newsletter* once told a story of a man in Liverpool, England,
who always chose the same set of lottery numbers. One time he forgot to
renew his ticket and "his" numbers came up. This poor man became so full
of self-recrimination and regret that he committed suicide. Mentally coming "this close" to a life of riches and then not getting it because of what he
didn't do was more than he could bear.

Do you ever put yourself in that vise? Do you replay events in your head
and think . . .

If only I'd just done that, things would be different.
If only I'd left the house ten minutes later.
If only I'd let him take my car, he wouldn't have run out of gas on a busy
  freeway.
If only I'd told him he had to return by ten.

The list never ends and it never stops punishing. But consider my bottom line on all the "if only's" of life:

God is in control.

God is sovereign.

When Christian was about ten, he went through a phase of worrying
about my traveling.

"What if your plane crashes, Mom?"

"What if someone breaks into your hotel room and hurts you?"

I'd pull out my Bible and take him to Psalm 139. If you ever struggle
with the what-if questions or feel uncertain and shaken in this world, then
copy this psalm and take it with you wherever you go.

O LORD, you have examined my heart
  and know everything about me.

You know when I sit down or stand up.

    You know my thoughts even when I'm far away.

You see me when I travel

    and when I rest at home.

    You know everything I do.

You know what I am going to say

    even before I say it, Lord.

You go before me and follow me.

    You place your hand of blessing on my head.

Such knowledge is too wonderful for me,

    too great for me to understand!

I can never escape from your Spirit!

    I can never get away from your presence!

If I go up to heaven, you are there;

    if I go down to the grave, you are there.

If I ride the wings of the morning,

    if I dwell by the farthest oceans, even there your hand will guide me,

    and your strength will support me.

I could ask the darkness to hide me

    and the light around me to become night—

    but even in darkness I cannot hide from you.

To you the night shines as bright as day.

    Darkness and light are the same to you.

You made all the delicate, inner parts of my body

    and knit me together in my mother's womb.

Thank you for making me so wonderfully complex! Your workmanship is

    marvelous—how well I know it.

You watched me as I was being formed in utter seclusion,

    as I was woven together in the dark of the womb.

You saw me before I was born.

    Every day of my life was recorded in your book.

Every moment was laid out
　　before a single day had passed. (Psalm 139:1–16, emphasis added)

I must have read that psalm to Christian a hundred times. Particularly verse 16. The word David used as he described God seeing him before he was born, called "unformed substance" in the ESV, is a word that only appears in this one place in the entire Old Testament. It translates "rolled" or "wrapped up." What a lovely description of an embryo or fetus wrapped tightly inside a mother's womb until God begins to unfold each part. David writes that every day of his life was recorded in God's book, referred to again in Psalm 69:28, where David calls out to God to punish his enemies, "Erase their names from the Book of Life; don't let them be counted among the righteous." The psalmist rests in this truth that God alone decided before he was born exactly how long he would live.

"Do you see, babe? Whether I travel or stay at home, God is with me. Before I was even born, every single moment of my life was written down. I won't go home to be with Jesus one day before or one day after Jesus says so."

This is a profound truth that we need to grasp hold of and own because the enemy would love to make us believe we live our lives on a tightrope, tentatively making our way over raging seas, never knowing when a gust of wind would knock us off. That is a lie. God is in control of all things at all times.

I often share this truth with those who are devastated by a tragic accident that takes the life of someone they dearly loved. Life can seem so random, so out of control, but even while our hearts are broken, there is a quiet confidence in knowing that although their death seems so untimely to us, to God they have finished their race. Do I understand why God allows certain terrible things to happen? I don't even pretend to. That's a huge subject that far more qualified writers than I have wrestled with. Nevertheless . . . I do find sweet rest in the truth that God is in control. As the psalmist wrote, "Our God is in heaven; he does whatever pleases him" (Psalm 115:3 NIV).

Can you embrace that truth too? Will you take the regrets of things you didn't do and lay them at Christ's feet? He sees your life. He watches over you. God's plan continues to unfold even when it feels out of control.

Things Done to You

Not long before Christmas one year, a friend's husband committed suicide, leaving his widow to raise three young children alone. No one in his closest circle saw it coming.

Suicide leaves those left behind with a multitude of emotions as they begin to survey the landscape that has been changed forever. A tornado often gives little warning; so, too, with suicide. I feel deep empathy for this family's tragedy, for my father took his own life at age thirty-four, leaving my mom to raise three children alone. A ruptured brain

Many women feel their lives have slipped into a freeze-frame, stopped cold at that moment, like a broken watch.

aneurysm had made him "not himself," and as a family we grew to understand that medical fact. But the desperate, agonizing part about suicide is that it closes the conversation. No matter how many questions you have or the anger you might feel . . . or regret you might have . . . the person is gone.

For some, divorce hits with a very similar punch. One day this man with whom you have shared your life says he no longer loves you. He walks out, doesn't look back, and carries on with his life. What are you supposed to do? I have talked to and wept with many women who feel as if their life has slipped into freeze-frame, stopped cold at that moment, like a broken watch. One woman wrote, "It's surreal, as if I'm in some terrible movie or bad dream that I can't wake up from. How can he just walk away and live a different life? What am I supposed to do?"

One of the harshest realities of life is that those we love don't always choose to stay on the journey with us.

I don't know what was going on with my friend's husband when he made his devastating choice to take his own life.

I don't know what thoughts went through my dad's mind before he slipped into the water.

I don't know why men (and women) at times walk away from everything and everyone they know and love and try to live a different life.

We just don't know. And I doubt that many of *them* truly understand it either. Was my friend's husband in so much pain in the chaos of that place that he chose a permanent solution for what might have been a passing storm? Those who have lived through a tornado say that it sounds like a freight train getting closer and closer with each passing second. I can only imagine the lies the enemy whispers as the sound of impending disaster approaches.

End it now!

Make it stop!

Take control!

The Prison of Regret

At times I've tried to imagine what might have been going on in my father's mind the night he took his life. He was only thirty-four years old and was confined to an asylum for the rest of his days. The damage that had been done to his brain was irreversible. Perhaps most cruel of all, he understood that. Because he had become violent before he was removed from our home, he was placed in the maximum security ward. He shared that dismal space with men in their seventies and eighties who had lost all touch with reality. That bittersweet gift was not given to my father.

There would be moments of clarity when he knew who he was, where he was, and what he had lost. My mother has told me that in those moments his wracking sobs were almost more than she could bear. So she asked my dad's doctor if he could be moved to a ward with some younger men. They moved him, but it was a less secure unit. On that first night my father escaped. They searched for him through the night and found him as morning broke.

He was caught in the salmon nets in the river.

Can you imagine the bitter regret my mother felt? Not only had she lost the only man she ever loved, but also she was the one who had asked if he could be moved. We never talked about these things when I was growing up. I don't know if it was Scottish reserve or just different times. But from the day of my father's funeral when I was five years old until I was in my thirties, we never spoke about what happened to my dad.

Ironically, it was only when I ended up in a psych ward at thirty-four that my personal tornado finally blew the roof off all our secrets. Mom flew over from Scotland and stayed in a hotel near the hospital so I wouldn't be alone when I was discharged. One morning my therapist invited her to share in one of my sessions. I had no way of knowing how terrible and beautiful that day would be. I had been so "careful" all my life with my family's emotions, particularly my mother's.

By the time I ended up in the hospital, however, all that was over. I was too bone-tired to try anymore. My therapist encouraged me to let my mother into the chaos of emotions I had struggled to manage for so long, convinced that one day they would pull me under. The questions poured out of me more in wails than in sentences. I was looking straight at her.

"Why did he do it?"

"Why did we never talk about him again?"

"Why did you blame me?"

A piercing sound filled the small office, and it came from my mother. I was shocked into silence.

There are parts of her story that are only hers to share. What I can say is wave after wave of regret *shook* her. She became a woman I had never met before.

For almost thirty years I thought my mom blamed me for my father's death while she had been blaming herself. It was devastating and beautiful to sit quietly as my therapist helped my mother see that she was no more to blame than I was.

Silent regret had rusted away years of shared comfort, forgiveness, and support. I can tell you today that for my mom and for me, God is a Redeemer.

Nothing is wasted.

Nothing is lost.

Nothing is missed.

King David reminds us that God gathers up our tears: "You keep track of all my sorrows. You have collected all my tears in your bottle. You have recorded each one in your book" (Psalm 56:8).

Others may not understand the weight of what you have wept, but God does.

Your life does not end when devastating circumstances threaten to consume you. The enemy, however, would love you to believe exactly that—that your life is wasted, over. He would love to make you live under the silent banner of REGRET for the rest of your life. Silent lies that we believe can cripple us.

Things Left Undone

My friend Christine Caine discovered in her thirties that her parents had adopted her. That same day she discovered that her brother had been adopted from a different mother. As her story began to unfold, the details became even more distressing.

Her birth certificate had reduced her to a number; the "name of child" line read "unnamed." The papers filled in by the social worker made it clear that her birth mother had little interest in this beautiful baby girl.

Unnamed. Unwanted.

Christine has the proof. I've seen the paperwork.

I've also seen a miracle.

I've watched this fiery Greek-Australian find a better source of facts about her life than some green folder in the bottom drawer of a file cabinet in some dreary government office. In the Word of God, she discovered that before she even entered her mother's womb, God knew her and had wonderful, meticulous plans for her. The idea of getting reduced to a number could have destroyed her, but instead, God has used that historical black-and-white fact to light a passionate fire inside her spirit.

Christine and her husband, Nick, head up a ministry called the A21 Campaign, a fight to end slavery in the twenty-first century. Did you know that more slaves populate the world today than at any other time in human history? More than twenty-seven million!

To Christine, not one of them is a number. Every one of them has a name, a future, and a precious life for which Christ died. Christine believes that each one is worth fighting for. (To find out more about Christine's work, check out her website.[1]) I consider Christine's life a stunningly beautiful picture of the way God thwarts the enemy's plans to destroy us. God loves to take what Satan intends for evil and instead use it for good!

I wonder what feels undone in your life? I don't know your hopes and dreams, or how someone may have pummeled them into the dust by leaving something undone. Perhaps you've waited for a long time for some guy to marry you, but he never makes a move in that direction. On a recent trip to London, I met a woman on a train who told me that she has been dating the same guy for thirteen years. She was in her forties now and was still waiting for him to ask her to marry him. I asked her if she had seen any signs of change, anything that would sustain her hope, but she said no. What had crippled her was that she believed she had already invested too much of her life waiting to simply walk away now.

"What if he never asks?" I said.

Her reply was heartbreaking. "He will. I know he will; he has to!"

Perhaps you've believed that your ex-husband would behave in a financially responsible way and help you raise your children, but month after month you get nothing but another excuse.

Take your deepest regrets to the cross. Own them. Allow yourself to feel the weight. The old English root of the word *regret* is *regrete*, which speaks of sorrow and lament. Speak out your sorrow and lamentation to your Father and let Him exchange what you cannot carry for what He has designed just for you. The Father's heart longs for all of us to move from the regret that paralyzes our souls to the deep rest that is found in Him. Unspoken regret can tarnish every sunrise, but it is not too late to throw the windows open and let the sunlight in.

I tore down the dark and dismal drapes that hung like dead men on the
   gallows.
I threw open the windows and cried out as sunlight spilled into this silent
   room as surprised as I.
And as my eyes became accustomed to this fierce and searching light,
I realized that it was time to laugh again.

—JOURNAL ENTRY

STANDING THROUGH YOUR STROM

Perhaps for the first time you are becoming aware of the weight of regret you have carried for so long and you are ready to break the silence.

1. *Be honest and own your regret.* Stuffing regret down into the basement of your soul will never deal with it. The enemy loves to rifle through regret and drag it back upstairs. Admit it, confess it, and ask Christ to forgive you for what you have done or left undone.

2. *Grieve your losses.* Allow yourself to feel the pain of things you wish had been, or once were. Even when the waves seem high, they will not consume you. Grieving hurts but also heals. Allow yourself to be human!

3. *Forgive.* Forgive yourself and those who played a part in the regrets of your past. Remember that when you forgive, *you* are the one set free.

4. *Ask God for the courage to fully engage in life again.* Don't allow the enemy to convince you that you have forfeited your part in the great, redemptive plan of God. The devil lies. You might want to buy a piece of scarlet ribbon and hang it in a place you see every day to remind you that God has delivered you, as surely as He delivered Rahab.

Almost a century and a half ago, the great Scottish churchman and poet Horatius Bonar penned some lines that continue to help me today. I pray they give the same comfort to you.

> When the weary, seeking rest,
> To Thy goodness flee;
> When the heavy laden cast
> All their load on Thee;
> When the troubled, seeking peace,
> On Thy Name shall call;
> When the sinner, seeking life,
> At Thy feet shall fall:
> Hear then in love, O Lord, the cry in Heav'n,
> Thy dwelling place on high.
> —*HYMNS OF FAITH AND HOPE*, 1866

Father God,

It feels as if I have been a prisoner of regret for so long that I forget what it feels like to be free. I ask You to help me unearth every regret, either for things I have done or for things that have been done to me and speak them out to You. I don't want to be a prisoner of this silent storm any longer. I choose to rest in You. I choose You!

Amen.

CHAPTER SIX

THUNDER AND LIGHTNING

FROM FEAR TO JOY

I'm not afraid of storms, for I'm learning how to sail my ship.
—LOUISE MAY ALCOTT, *LITTLE WOMEN*

*"Let not your hearts be troubled. Believe in God; believe also in me.
In my Father's house are many rooms. If it were not so, would I have
told you that I go to prepare a place for you? And if I go and prepare
a place for you, I will come again and will take you to myself, that
where I am you may be also."*

—JOHN 14:1–3 (ESV)

I had five minutes before the closing of the plane door, so I quickly checked my text messages before turning off my phone.

One from Barry said, "Call me when you land in Denver. I love you!"

Another from Christian said, "Mom, can Dylan spend the night?"

But the one from Sally, one of the vice presidents at Women of Faith (a conference for women that I've been a part of since 1996), made my heart skip a beat. She had received news that a woman in Denver who held tickets to our event there had just been brutally murdered. She had no further information.

I had a hard time absorbing it all.

My jumbled thoughts got interrupted by the familiar, "Please turn off all BlackBerrys, iPhones, iPads, Kindles, anything with an on-and-off switch."

I shot Sally a quick text before they closed the plane door: "If there is anything I can do when I get there, please let me know."

My mind raced. What had happened to this poor woman? She clearly hadn't died in an accident. Sally had spoken of a brutal murder. Did she die in a domestic dispute? In some random act of violence?

I thought of the promise given in the final conversation Jesus had with His closest friends. I meditate often on this text, a favorite of mine: "I am leaving you with a gift—peace of mind and heart. And the peace I give is a gift the world cannot give. So don't be troubled or afraid" (John 14:27).

While every promise of Christ is rock solid, I admit that, at times, I struggle with holding the truth of His promise in one hand and balancing it against the harsh realities of our world in the other. Terrible, unthinkable things happen to innocent people on our planet. Violence invades sleepy communities and changes their landscape forever. And now that violence had visited another little town in Colorado.

By the time my plane touched down in Denver, I had several messages from Women of Faith staff members filling me in on what had happened. I learned the name of the murdered woman: Mary Katherine Ricard. She had worked as a prison guard at Arkansas Valley Correctional Facility in Ordway, Colorado. One text message contained a link to an article in the *Denver Post*. When I pulled up the piece, its headline grabbed my heart: "Mary Katherine Ricard would have had forgiveness for her killer." The rest of the article offered a few details of the crime. Mary had died swiftly and violently in the prison kitchen, where she supervised inmate cooks.

I sat for a while in the terminal before I walked to baggage claim. The news made me sick at heart. I prayed for Mary's daughter, for all her family, and for the prison staff. It must devastate them all when a fellow officer dies violently in the line of duty.

I called home to see if Barry had heard the news. He had. Someone from our staff had contacted the deceased's family, and Barry now had the cell number of Mary Katherine's daughter, Katie. He told me that he had spoken with her for a few moments and had a little more information about the murder.

"Katie told me her mom never worked Mondays," Barry said. "She was supposed to be on duty this Friday night, but she changed shifts because she wanted to hear you speak on Friday night, Sheila. She was murdered on Monday night."

I sat with tears rolling down my face as I thought about this mom and daughter making plans and changing schedules so they could worship with us at Women of Faith. Mary got up that morning and went to work, believing that she had made it possible to enjoy some mom-daughter time.

I wanted to reach out in some way to the family, but what do you say in the face of such senseless violence? With grief so fresh, it's hard to know what to do. Sometimes people just want to grieve alone and in private.

"Do you think I should call?" I asked.

"Yes," Barry said, "she asked if you would call."

I waited for the quiet and privacy of my hotel room. I got down on my knees and prayed a prayer that has become very familiar to me over the years. "Lord Jesus Christ, I kneel at Your feet one more time, holding out what I have inside and offering it to You. It is clearly not enough for this situation. So I ask You to take the loaves and fishes of my life, and bless them and break them and feed Your broken people."

I dialed the number and Katie answered. We talked for a few moments, then Katie asked if she could put me on speakerphone.

"My dad and brother and some of the rest of my family are here. Do you have any words for us?"

I read a psalm that has brought me comfort countless times.

> The LORD is my shepherd;
>> I have all that I need.

He lets me rest in green meadows;
> he leads me beside peaceful streams.
He renews my strength.
He guides me along right paths,
> bringing honor to his name.
Even when I walk
> through the darkest valley,
> I will not be afraid,
> > for you are close beside me.
Your rod and your staff
> protect and comfort me.
You prepare a feast for me
> in the presence of my enemies.
You honor me by anointing my head with oil.
My cup overflows with blessings.
Surely your goodness and unfailing love will pursue me
> all the days of my life,
and I will live in the house of the LORD
> forever. (Psalm 23)

Then I prayed. I prayed for comfort, for strength, and for the peace of Christ that defies explanation. Katie told me that for the last several years she and her mom had attended our conferences together. "We looked forward to it every year," she said. "It was our time for spiritual renewal. We always laughed a lot and cried a lot, but we left with real joy."

Before we hung up, I asked Katie if I could do anything for her or for the family. She told me that on the following Monday, a memorial service for her mom would be held. Three thousand corrections officers would fly in from around the country.

"My mom loved when you sang 'You Raise Me Up,'" she said. "Would you stay over and sing that at her service?"

"Of course I will."

The family remained in my thoughts and prayers all that weekend. I wondered about those last moments for Mary Katherine. Did she try to fight back? While raw fear can spur us into acts of what seem like superhuman strength, sometimes it simply paralyzes us.

When I was sixteen years old, I saw a car strike a woman and her baby as they used a pedestrian crossing. The car hit the baby stroller so hard that the infant flew into the air like a ragdoll, while the car dragged the mother several feet. Although I stood only a few feet away, I remained riveted in place. Even as others rushed past me to help, I did nothing. I couldn't even look. I stood at the edge of the road with my face buried in my hands. I couldn't move. I remember hearing a strange whining noise and wondering what it could be—until I realized the noise came from me. For months I felt deeply ashamed of my inability to do anything but stand there, paralyzed with fear.

Have you ever had a moment like that? Perhaps not as dramatic as watching an accident unfold before your eyes, but a moment when fear gripped you and you felt its steel-cold bands wrap around your heart and mind.

THE MANY FACES OF FEAR

Fear comes in many guises. It can be as sudden and violent as lightning striking a tree and splitting it in half or as perpetual and debilitating as day after day of rain with no promise of sunshine. For many of us, fear is a response to an unexpected situation, but for others it feels like part of the fabric of their souls.

I have a friend who checks several times a night to make sure her baby is breathing. The possibility of losing her little one torments her and robs her of sleep. She will admit that her fear has no rational basis. Her baby is strong and healthy, but fear shadows everything in her life like ominous internal thunderclouds.

You might categorize your own fear as anxiety. But while the reality of fear is different for each of us, one thing remains constant: fear robs us of joy. When fear takes center stage, we find it impossible to live in the "what is" because of the "what might be."

Anxiety has reached epidemic proportions in America. Despite its status as the richest nation on earth, the United States also has the dubious distinction of being the most anxious, with nearly a third of Americans likely to suffer from an anxiety problem in their lifetime.[1] No other nation even comes close.

Where does this anxiety and fear originate? Some say our national pursuit of happiness leads to inordinate and desperate unhappiness. We feel consumed by a search for an elevated state of being that simply doesn't exist—or, at least, not for long—on this earth.

That certainly sounds plausible, but then why do so many of us who love God feel overwhelmed by fear?

Just before Christmas I spoke at an event in a small town in Texas with the evocative name Dripping Springs. I asked the women in attendance what gifts they would lay at the manger for the Christ child had they been there on that holy night so long ago. I expected some of the answers:

"I would give Him my heart."

"I would give Him all my love."

But I found some of the answers quite surprising and even very revealing. Several cards spoke to a deep brokenness and fear of the future.

"I would give Him my anxiety."

"I would give my fear of the future."

"I would give Him my children; I'm afraid for their future."

"I would give Him my marriage. I would ask Him to bring my husband home."

"I would give Him everything I have if He would just give me peace."

The enemy loves to use the weapon of fear against us, finely honing it to pierce the hearts of God's daughters. We read in Scripture that perfect love casts out fear (1 John 4:18 ESV), but somehow we have a hard time relating to that word *perfect*. Our hearts long to know just how that might work out in practice.

THUNDER AND LIGHTNING

Think back to the beginning of this chapter. Did you wonder, at least a little, why I would choose to begin a meditation on overcoming fear with the story of a woman who loved God but who lost her life at the hands of a murderer? I picked the story for a very simple reason: if the love of God can overpower the worst the enemy can throw at us, then we don't have to fear his vilest attempts at destroying us. When we dare to look full in the face at the worst life has to offer, and yet even in there see the redemptive mercy of God, then fear must take a backseat in our lives—or get out and walk far behind. It has an inevitable place on our journey, but it doesn't get to dictate the road ahead.

Yes, that weekend in Denver began with shocking, horrific news. As the events of the following days unfolded, however, God broke through, like a sudden shaft of sunlight piercing the dark clouds. On the day of Mary Katherine's memorial service, He showed me the power of the cross over fear in a way I had never witnessed before. God took what the enemy meant to destroy this family and brought true joy out of what began as terror.

On reflection, I don't know what I expected such a memorial service would be like, but I could not have anticipated the palpable climate change God's Spirit produced in that high school auditorium. God owned this tribute to His beautiful daughter and painted a picture of the pure joy of a redeemed life over the canvas of what to human eyes seemed only one more meaningless tragedy.

I got there early that morning. I wanted to watch and pray as the correction officers began to stream in. I knew from Katie that her mom had previously worked as a chef in a fabulous restaurant at one of Colorado's premier ski resorts but had taken this job at the prison so she could bring the light and life of Christ into such a dark and hopeless place. Now she was gone. I knew deep in my gut that the enemy was rejoicing at the senseless violence he had stirred up in a moment. One lightning strike and she was down. I prayed with everything in me, "God, redeem this bloody ground."

The silence was profound as row after row of officers filed into the auditorium. I could tell by the badges on their uniforms where they served. There were men and women from every state, from New York to Los Angeles. The last of the officers to take their seats were from the prison where Mary Katherine had served. Then the family was escorted in. The atmosphere was heavy as if thunderclouds had slipped in the back door and hovered threateningly over every head.

The service was about to begin when Katie slipped over to where I was sitting and said, "Before you sing, would you say a few words about what mattered to my mom?"

As I walked to the podium, I looked at Mary Katherine's photograph surrounded by flowers, such a sweet smile on her face; my sister in Christ, she had finished her race. I looked at the faces of this somber crowd and told them that earth has a different system of paperwork than heaven. On that Monday, when Mary Katherine's body ceased to breathe, our paperwork would indicate that her life had come to an end. But in heaven, on that glorious homecoming day, the paperwork would read, "Welcome home. Well done, good and faithful servant!"

I paused and then the music began to play for the song I was asked to sing. Halfway through, something happened. When I came to the words "You raise me up so I can stand on mountains," Katie stood and raised her hands in worship. Then Mary Katherine's husband, Tim, stood and raised his hands in worship, with tears rolling down his face. Soon, all across the auditorium, men and women in uniform stood. I don't know why some stood. I'm sure some in respect, but others raised their hands, too, worshipping the One who holds the keys of death and hell, the One no prison bars could hold or tomb contain.

Katie's and Tim's choice to stand, knowing that Mary Katherine was home free, was breathtaking. God threw the doors open, and the thunderclouds of what was true for a moment was banished by what is true eternally. Mary Katherine won! She was home free.

Clearly most of life is lived out in less dramatic moments, but no matter the intensity of the fear that we will all face from time to time, the truth remains that it can place a stranglehold on joy. The feelings of fear can be immobilizing. So let's take a look at what the Bible has to say about fear, its different forms and its roots.

The enemy does not possess the wisdom of our God. For that reason, he often overplays his hand. What he intends to use to destroy us, God uses to make us strong and to give us a joy that is deeper and eternal.

FEAR IN GOD'S WORD

Fear can enter through many different doors. Disobedience to God naturally results in fear. After Adam sinned and God asked him for an explanation for his evil behavior, the guilty man replied, "I heard you walking in the garden, so I hid. I was afraid because I was naked" (Genesis 3:10).

On the other end of the spectrum, a reverent kind of fear can indicate an appropriate response to God's holy judgment: "By faith Noah, being warned by God concerning events as yet unseen, in reverent fear constructed an ark for the saving of his household. By this he condemned the world and became an heir of the righteousness that comes by faith" (Hebrews 11:7 ESV).

We ought to feel a very natural and life-preserving kind of fear when something threatens our well-being or continued existence: "Then the sailors bound ropes around the hull of the ship to strengthen it. They were afraid of being driven across to the sandbars of Syrtis off the African coast, so they lowered the sea anchor to slow the ship and were driven before the wind" (Acts 27:17).

We know, too, that when the Son of Man returns in power and great glory, many will respond in terror: "People will be terrified at what they see coming upon the earth, for the powers in the heavens will be shaken. Then everyone will see the Son of Man coming on a cloud with power and great glory. So when all these things begin to happen, stand and look up, for your salvation is near!" (Luke 21:26–28).

Not so for those of us who love Christ. Jesus Christ, who conquered death, delivers us from the fear of death: "Because God's children are human beings—made of flesh and blood—the Son also became flesh and blood. For only as a human being could he die, and only by dying could he break the power of the devil, who had the power of death. Only in this way could he set free all who have lived their lives as slaves to the fear of dying" (Hebrews 2:14–15).

Fear of death, or the fear of the process of dying, has plagued humanity since the fall in Eden. Satan keeps it in easy reach within his arsenal and counts it as one of his most potent weapons against us. When he tempted Adam and Eve to disobey God, his plan was to destroy them and to destroy their relationship with God forever. But his arrogance blinded him to the truth that God had and always has had a much bigger plan. It is this "much bigger plan" that I would like us to consider more deeply.

It's clear that bad things can happen in this world. Those of us who love God are not immune from life's pain. But when the tidal wave of fear approaches, we need to remember that because of the sacrifice of Christ we have been redeemed. Satan cannot follow us beyond this life. God has said, "This far and no farther." Even when we face situations that are overwhelming, we have a place to take our fear. As David wrote, "When I am afraid, I put my trust in you" (Psalm 56:3 ESV).

A Trail of Blood

I wonder when Satan first began to suspect that his plan to destroy all that God loves had some major problems.

Once he successfully goaded Adam and Eve into sinning, he knew he had broken our perfect relationship with God. Can you imagine how he must have roared with delight as he watched Adam and Eve evicted from the garden, clothed by God in animal skins? He had no idea that this tragic picture of loss and banishment was part of God's plan to redeem us all. The animal blood that was shed in Eden to cover Adam and Eve was just the beginning, a pointer to the blood that would one day be shed to cover us all.

All Satan saw was death and defeat; he could not have imagined that the skins represented a perfect Lamb to come who would save us. He didn't realize that God had already begun to send us on our way home. When Satan saw blood, it spoke of death, but when God sheds blood, it speaks of life. I wonder if Satan paid any attention to the warning in the garden that day? God told him that one day the seed of a woman to come would crush his head, even as he bruised His heel. But the smell of blood was in the air, and his outworking of his evil had just begun.

Next, the devil whispered his insidious lies to Cain, the oldest son of Adam and Eve: "God seems much more pleased with your brother's offering than with yours. I wonder—why is *he* the favored one? Doesn't that just make you hate him?"

Satan watched as Cain slaughtered his brother, Abel, then tried to hide what he had done from God. But God told Cain, "Your brother's blood cries out to me from the ground!" (Genesis 4:10).

For Satan, another triumph. Death had become a part of human life.

The trail of man shedding the blood of his fellow man that began with Cain winds its way down through the centuries through all types of betrayal, plotting, fights, and murder. Many good men and women resisted the devil's deadly whispers—Noah, Abraham, Sarah, Ruth, Samuel, Abigail, Hezekiah—but those who listened to the homicidal lies of the enemy always outnumbered them.

And then the pages of the Old Testament closed . . . silence. No word from God for four hundred years.

We don't have a biblical record of living conditions for those Israelites who populated the land during God's silence from the end of the Old until the beginning of the New Testament. We don't know what evils Satan and his legions perpetrated during that time. His wicked nature does not change, however, so we can safely guess he did everything possible to fuel darkness, deceit, and despair. Tidal waves of fear must have washed over the lives of those who wondered if God had forgotten them. But in faith, many would have stood and looked to the horizon because God had made a promise of a coming Messiah and God cannot lie.

And then one night a star appeared in the eastern sky. A Jewish baby cried out in the darkness. Nothing about the child or His parents warranted much devilish attention, other than a few wide-eyed shepherds who made their way to a stable and then began to spread some wild stories about the baby. And yet . . . it was Bethlehem. Hadn't the prophet Micah stated that one was coming who would lead God's flock and he would be born in Bethlehem (Micah 5:2)?

Months passed, the boy grew, and He and His parents vacated a stable and occupied a house. About that time, some rich foreigners arrived at Herod's palace, looking for the boy whom they said had been born to be King.

Something is wrong, Satan thought, *but what, exactly?* He could take no chances that this was the one who would crush his head, so he whispered his most venomous lies into the corrupt heart of Herod, who ordered the slaughter of every baby boy in Bethlehem two years old and younger. Soldiers spilled a lot of blood that night, but for the enemy the blood was spilled in vain; the Christ child already had departed. An angel had warned Joseph in a dream to leave for Egypt, and he obediently took Mary and her son to safety in the south.

Time passed, and one day a common man emerged from the baptismal waters of the Jordan River. At that moment *something* happened in the heavens—a voice, God's voice, made an announcement that chilled the dark heart of the fallen cherub who once had led worship in heaven. Satan would have to watch this man.

The devil toyed with Christ in the wilderness for forty days. He threw his best at Him, things that for thousands of years had caused great men to fall—but Jesus didn't fall. And He refused to bow. Instead, He used the Word of God against the enemy of God. Satan then left Him . . . for a time.

The devil watched as he saw the man becoming popular, too popular. People who had forgotten what it was like to be in relationship with God started turning to God and pledging to follow Him and His ways.

That was when Satan knew he would have to call upon his favorite, most trusted weapon. If this man would not bow to him, then He would have to die.

The enemy tried to get the crowds to kill Jesus—stone Him, throw Him off a cliff, or get rid of Him in some other way—but none of his schemes worked. He had no idea that death was God's plan all along. Nothing in the darkest self-serving recesses of evil could have alerted Satan to the shocking truth that the Father would ask the Son to lay down His life. Perfect love casts out fear, but when there is only perfect hatred, the thought of sacrificial love would not even exist. So the enemy continued to push for the death of Jesus and came up with what must have seemed like the perfect plan, the ultimate slap in the face of God.

Let's use the religious leaders, he determined. *What a perfect end, to bring Him down at the hands of those who are supposed to represent Him on this earth!* The irony was laden with sadistic pleasure. He used some of his favorite darts on the puffed-up ones—pride, self-righteousness, envy, and anger—and it worked. They manipulated the system to have Jesus crucified.

I wonder where in the crowd Satan stood that day when Christ, the perfect Lamb of God, was spread out for the world to see, blood dripping to the ground? But however close he approached, the devil missed it again. He failed to put two and two together. He didn't see the common link—the animal blood in the garden, the lamb's blood on the doorpost, the Lamb of God's blood on Calvary. His pride and arrogance had swollen his eyes shut.

For Satan, this dark moment justified everything. His rebellion had succeeded, ending where it had begun:

I am greater!

I am wiser!

I win!

As he watched Christ die, one statement alone must have convinced him that he had won. He had listened with loathing as Jesus asked His Father to forgive. He despised the exchange between Christ, His mother, and John, but then he heard this: "My God, my God, why have you forsaken me?" (Matthew 27:46 ESV). That was when he knew he had done the impossible; he was as magnificent as he always declared himself to be, for he had defeated God.

Christ breathed His last, and everyone but a few foolish women scattered to the four winds. Evening and morning, evening and morning, and all remained silent. Before dawn even started coloring the sky on that second morning, perhaps he was there and watched those women return to anoint Christ's battered body with myrrh and other spices. *Too little, too late,* Satan must have thought. Myrrh, one of the three gifts the kings had given to Mary. If frankincense spoke of the presence of God with His people, myrrh should have warned them: he's not going to survive this.

But then Mary reached an empty tomb.

No! It cannot be!

But it was. Jesus stood there, very much alive. He had risen from the dead!

When do you suppose Satan realized that the very thing he had orchestrated had instead accomplished the very plan of God? We know only that he had no inkling that the greatest mistake he ever made was crucifying Jesus. How do we know that? Look at 1 Corinthians 2:7–8:

> No, the wisdom we speak of is the mystery of God—his plan that was previously hidden, even though he made it for our ultimate glory before the world began. But the rulers of this world have not understood it; if they had, they would not have crucified our glorious Lord.

Do you see the pure, undiluted triumphant joy of God's plan right from the very beginning, even before Adam and Eve fell! God knew the enemy would do everything he could to destroy us all . . . but God had a plan in place. Before time began the Lord determined that Christ would come and die for you and me, that He would rise again, and that Satan and all his demonic hordes would come to a ruinous, final defeat. If Satan had understood that crucifying Jesus was God's plan all along, he would have done everything in his power to stop it. Instead of whispering the name of Barabbas into the minds of the bloodthirsty crowd gathered before Pilate, he would have whispered the name of Jesus.

Satan is a defeated enemy, and the sands of time are running out for him—and he knows it. What does he have left? Only his lies, his hatred, and a limited number of days, known only to God.

Defeated does not mean "destroyed," however, and his attacks still hit with great effectiveness. *Defeated* tells us that his days are numbered, but as long as he still has one day left, we are not immune from his attacks. And yet God has given us clear instruction in His Word as to how we should live in these days.

STAND STRONG

Too often we forget Paul's many admonitions to watch out for the enemy, to remain vigilant for his attacks. Every day of our lives Satan prowls around this earth, desiring nothing more than to get God's children to fall. Our eyes cannot see the astonishing intensity of the battle raging around us. So Paul encourages us to stand strong, reminding us that God has not left us defenseless:

> A final word: Be strong in the Lord and in his mighty power. Put on all of God's armor so that you will be able to stand firm against all strategies of the devil. For we are not fighting against flesh-and-blood enemies, but against evil rulers and authorities of the unseen world, against mighty powers in this dark world, and against evil spirits in the heavenly places. (Ephesians 6:10–12)

This chapter promised a shift from fear to joy, and perhaps you don't yet quite grasp how that is possible. "If our enemy still has power, even though limited and restrained by God," you may ask, "then how can I know joy now? Perhaps joy belongs to a future age, one devoid of the devil's presence?" What Paul is telling us in the above passage is that we should be afraid if we have been left defenseless but we have not. Paul wrote, "Therefore, put on every piece of God's armor so you will be able to resist the enemy in the time of evil. Then after the battle you will still be standing firm." That is the promise—you will still be standing firm! (Read Ephesians 6:13–17 for a detailed list of the armor.)

Yes, the enemy will rage and thunder over our lives, but God's lightning strike on the cross dealt fear and death a fatal blow.

Just before His arrest, Jesus told His grieving followers, "I will see you again and you will rejoice, and *no one will take away your joy*" (John 16:22 NIV, emphasis added). Here Christ is speaking of resurrection joy. The resurrection of Christ changed everything for the disciples, for Mary Katherine, for you, and for me. Yes, we will lose some battles on this earth, but because Christ is not a dead leader but a risen Savior, we have a joy that no one can steal. Our happiness is impacted by our circumstances but our joy is secure in Christ.

Not only would Jesus' resurrection give His followers the ability to live with joy in this *present* age, but Jesus prayed that they might experience the *same* kind of joy that He Himself did. Incredible! Listen to His prayer in the Upper Room:

> "I am coming to you now, but I say these things while I am still in the world, so that they may have the full measure of my joy within them." (John 17:13 NIV)

And how can we have "the full measure" of Christ's joy within us? First, we must understand that joy is much greater than happiness. Happiness can come and go in a moment, but the joy Christ had and that He promises to us is a deep-rooted conviction that we win in the end, even if we have to suffer here on earth.

Yes, we will face some rough storms that may displace happiness for a season, but they cannot rob us of the joy that the cross declares: He is risen! We will be still be afraid at times, sure. But when I feel the thundercloud of fear begin to roll over me, I remember Christ's words to Mary on the resurrection morning, "Who are you looking for?" It might seem like an obvious question but in reality it is a life-changing question.

When you are afraid for your children, who are you looking for?

When you fear what might happen to our nation's economy, who are you looking for?

When you receive a diagnosis you didn't see coming, who are you looking for?

The presence of the risen Christ changes everything. We may lose a few battles along the way, but we win the war, girls! Anything the enemy can throw in our faces has a *very* short shelf life. Its "sell by" date has almost expired.

Can you grasp this glorious truth?

Many moments on earth will break our hearts. We will have to wear many labels in this life that we would never choose for ourselves. But never forget that *none* of them are eternal. What happens to us throughout our entire lives is but "for a season" in the glorious, eternal time line God has for us. That's a second key to experiencing joy on this earth.

You may have cancer for a season; you do not have cancer eternally.

You may have lost a child for a season; you have not lost a child eternally.

Katie may have lost her mother for a season; she has not lost her mother eternally.

Martin Luther captured this noble truth so profoundly in his great hymn "A Mighty Fortress":

> And though this world, with devils filled,
> Should threaten to undo us,
> We will not fear, for God hath willed
> His truth to triumph through us:
> The Prince of Darkness grim,
> We tremble not for him;
> His rage we can endure,
> For lo, his doom is sure,
> One little word shall fell him.
> That word above all earthly powers,
> No thanks to them, abideth;
> The Spirit and the gifts are ours

Through Him who with us sideth:
Let goods and kindred go,
This mortal life also;
The body they may kill:
God's truth abideth still,
His kingdom is forever.

God's kingdom and your joy last forever. "Weeping may stay for the night," wrote the psalmist, "but rejoicing comes in the morning" (Psalm 30:5 NIV). And the morning of God's final kingdom has no end.

You Raise Me Up

A few months after Mary Katherine's memorial service, I was speaking at a church in Colorado Springs, and I invited Katie to spend the day with me as my guest. I wanted to know how she was doing now that all the press had moved on and life for others had returned to normal. Obviously she was still heartbroken over her mother's brutal murder, but what I saw in Katie's eyes that day was a confident joy in knowing that what Satan intended for evil, God was continuing to use for good. "My mom wanted her life to make a difference. She just didn't know it was going to be this big! People are still talking about her service."

As I write, I have in front of me the simple order of service from that day, Monday, October 1, 2012. The last thing written on it comes from Psalm 23. One line in particular stands out: "Even though I walk through the valley of the shadow of death I will fear no evil, for you are with me."

Jesus does not promise you a perpetually happy life, but He does promise you a depth of joy equal to His own . . . which is very great.

Although you will suffer loss in this life, that loss is *temporary*.

We are not home yet, dear friend, but one day soon, we will be! So tuck this memory verse deep into a crevice of your heart, where the winds of circumstance will never blow it away.

"I am leaving you with a gift—peace of mind and heart. And the peace I give is a gift the world cannot give. So don't be troubled or afraid." (John 14:27)

STANDING THROUGH YOUR STORM

There will come moments in life when you will be asked to walk through such a shadowed valley. You will face situations where fear threatens to paralyze you. In those moments you need to do four things:

1. Find a place where you can get alone with Jesus.

2. Hear Him speak these words that He spoke to His closest friends, just before His arrest: "The peace I give is a gift the world cannot give. So don't be troubled or afraid" (John 14:27).

3. When the storm inside seems ready to consume you, remember that the One who calms the storm is very much alive and very much with you.

4. When the sky is dark and you are struggling to see, hear Christ ask you, "Who are you looking for?" Respond with joy, "For You, Lord. I am looking for You!"

Lord Jesus Christ,

I will never know all You faced on that brutal cross, but I thank You for taking my place so I can be free. Thank You that the enemy is defeated. Thank You that You alone hold the keys of death and hell. Teach me to find You when fear darkens my heart so that Your joy will be my strength.

Amen.

CHAPTER SEVEN

BATTERED TO BEAUTIFUL

FROM INSECURITY TO CONFIDENCE

*I hate the thought that I'm just some kind of Russian nesting doll
with the big outside and inevitably, rattling around under all the
layers, a crude little peg with a face is the truth of me.*
— WENDY MCCLURE, *I'M NOT THE NEW ME*

*If you think you are standing strong, be careful not to fall. The
temptations in your life are no different from what others experience.
And God is faithful. He will not allow the temptation to be more
than you can stand. When you are tempted, he will show you a way
out so that you can endure.*
— 1 CORINTHIANS 10:12–13

I nterviewers often ask me two questions that I struggle to answer:

"Tell us something funny that's happened to you onstage."

"Tell us something about yourself that we don't know."

As to the first, well . . . define *funny*. What might sound funny to one
person can offend or upset another. During a live radio interview, someone

once asked me the first question and my mind went completely blank. The interviewer appeared to have no desire to rescue me and simply waited for me to dig up some hilarious moment from my life on the road. Nobody likes dead air on radio, so I frantically ransacked though the files in my head, like a guilty party summoned into the IRS for an audit. Eventually I grabbed something and ran with it.

"One time," I related, "a bird got caught in a fan above me onstage and bits of wing and leg and feathers landed on my head. That was quite . . . funny."

Apparently not. Turns out that "dead air" can get even deader.

My second most challenging question came up more recently.

"Sheila, tell us something about yourself that our audience doesn't know."

Since I was on television this time, at least I could occupy the silence by looking as if I were studiously mulling over the question. Actually, several thoughts collided in my head:

> *I wonder if there is a Starbucks near here.*
> *I wonder if the bird story might work better on television.*

But something else came out of my mouth: "I talk to myself. I talk to myself a lot." I'm not sure it was the kind of revelation the interviewer sought, but at least it had the merit of being true.

I *do* talk a lot to myself, and not just in my head. I talk out loud. It's one reason I like having pets, because when I walk down the street with my dogs, onlookers assume I'm talking to them, even though I'm actually talking to myself. It took my husband some time to get used to this quirky personal trait. He kept trying to join this private conversation, which ultimately confused us both. Me, myself, and I don't like being interrupted.

Now, let me clarify (before you suggest I up my medication). I don't do this all the time. I do it when I'm trying to process something. It helps me think with more clarity. If I have a very busy day, I'll walk through the kitchen, saying, "Okay, take the dogs out first, then go to the post office and the grocery store. No, don't do that. Leave the grocery store to last or the ice cream will melt." You get the drift.

You may not talk out loud to yourself, but we all have conversations going on in our heads. You might be having lunch with a friend you haven't seen for some time, and as the sunlight threatens to blind you as it bounces off her new fire-engine-red hair color, there may well be a little conversation going on internally. Perhaps it takes some self-talk before you can get up in that meeting at work and deliver your report. Some of your internal conversation might be very pleasant as you stand in front of a mirror and admire yourself in a new outfit. (This clearly never applies to bathing suits.)

But I know, too, some of our internal monologues are quite devastating and ugly.

> *Why did you eat that? You're so fat!*
> *You can't wear that . . . you look terrible!*
> *Why did you say that?*
> *I don't belong here.*
> *She doesn't like me.*
> *Why is my husband looking at her?*

An incessant stream of negative feedback floods our minds and hearts. Think about the last time you looked in one of those unholy magnified mirrors. What thoughts immediately came to mind? Would you characterize them as largely positive or almost always negative?

We seem to have an innate desire to put ourselves down. Have you noticed how we tend to respond even to compliments?

"I love your dress!"

"What, this old thing?"

"Did you do something new with your hair? It looks great."

"I needed to cover the grey!"

"Your son is such a sweet boy!"

"You should see him at home!"

This pattern of deflecting compliments can become so ingrained that we don't even recognize it. I've worked with the same production crew at arena events for several years. One Friday evening after I'd spoken, I rode the crew bus back to the hotel with a couple of the camera guys and our worship team. As one of the girls passed me to find a seat, she commented on how much she had enjoyed my message. I thanked her and made some passing "funny" comment.

The camera operator sitting behind me immediately asked me, "Why do you always do that?"

"Do what?" I asked.

"Every time a woman tells you that God used you or that your message touched her, you find a way of sidelining the compliment," he stated.

His comment struck home; truth has a way of doing that. And I realized I've always found it very hard to accept personally affirming words. Some of that comes from growing up in Scotland, a culture that views encouragement and affirmation as a mild form of poison. *It might go to her head!*

But the larger part I can trace to a conviction already formed by the time I turned six. I thought of myself as essentially *wrong*. Whenever someone said something kind or affirming to me, I deflected the comment. I reasoned that he or she simply didn't know me well enough to see the truth. The speaker didn't know the *real me*.

OLD WOUNDS, RE-INFLICTED

How hard we can be on ourselves! Some of the verbal daggers that pierce our hearts come from wounds suffered long ago. Left untreated, they will hound us for years, and they easily get re-inflicted on others.

On a recent flight home from a speaking engagement, I almost came unglued with a mother sitting across the aisle from me. Her little son looked to be about five years old. Five times she called this darling little boy "stupid." I felt every dagger going in. At one point I put my hand on her arm and asked if I could get her anything, but she simply turned her inner fury in my direction. With one cold, steely look, she silenced me.

My heart ached for that little boy, and honestly for the woman too. What had happened to her? The storm raging inside her was deadly. I could only imagine the damage she had already inflicted on this tender heart. Was she simply blasting him with the same hail that had bruised her as a child? How did this little one feel inside—worthless, unloved, shamed to his core? I prayed for him. I imagined what his future would look like apart from the grace and mercy of God (and some good counseling).

Words cut deep, and none cut deeper than those from a parent. I have talked to grown men blessed with successful careers who still hear those death-row words playing in their heads from decades—or even half a century—in the past: *You are so stupid! You look so awkward. You'll never amount to anything.*

A friend of mine has enjoyed great success as a lecturer and teacher. All her students love her; in fact, you have to sign up early to make sure you get into her classes. Everyone considers her a sharp, classy, and elegant woman; but throughout her life, she has carried with her the terrible words she heard from her father as a little girl: "You are not pretty, but you are smart." How does that make a woman feel? In a culture that places so much value on image, it told my friend, "You'd better be good at what you do because that's all you've got to offer."

I have struggled with self-image issues my whole life. I had my first real boyfriend at age sixteen. I felt so excited that someone as popular as he would choose someone like me. But his idea of what it meant to have a girlfriend turned out to be worlds apart from mine. At a birthday party for one of our classmates, he attempted to unbutton my blouse. I pushed him away, horrified—and he dropped me that night, like a piece of trash. By the next day, word had spread all around school that I was, as he put it, "a frigid little nun." I felt humiliated. It seemed as though everywhere I went, people in little groups were talking about me.

Scotland long ago ceased to be a God-fearing nation; in fact, less than 2 percent of our population still attends church. Even back then, I was the only one in my high school class who publicly acknowledged a relationship with Christ. I knew many of my friends and classmates thought it amusing that "Sheila loves Jesus," but the incident at the party became the final casting vote that sent me off the island. I was not to be a survivor. I was different, and different was not good.

It didn't bother me so much that he had dropped me because I had refused to comply with his raging hormonal wishes. As a follower of Christ, my behavior mattered to me. What cut so deep was the look in his eyes and in the eyes of so many others. They all sent me the silent message, *You don't belong and you never will.*

Where Do You Feel Insecure?

Spend a little time reflecting on your own life. Did you have any moments like the ones I just described?

Childhood offers lot of opportunities for deep wounding. We can spend most of our school years dodging a series of emotional land mines that threaten to detonate and devastate us. In Scotland, we played a game called Red Rover. The game would begin with two team leaders calling out the names of those whom they wanted to join their team.

"Red rover, red rover, we want Sally to come over!"

This process went on until everyone had been chosen. But the last person wasn't chosen so much as inflicted on the team—the only person left, the residue, the unwelcome.

Bottom of the barrel
Not wanted
Not loved
Not chosen

Some moments in childhood leave us with a limp, but others feel so devastating they leave us crippled.

The National Center for Victims of Crime, the nation's leading resource and advocacy organization for crime victims, reports some very disturbing statistics about the United States.

- One out of five girls and one out of twenty boys is a victim of childhood sexual abuse.
- Twenty-eight percent of American young people between the ages of fourteen and seventeen have been sexually victimized.
- Children are the most vulnerable to sexual abuse between the ages of seven and thirteen. Perhaps most tragic of all, three out of four of those abused were victimized by someone they knew and trusted.
- Children who suffer sexual abuse are thirteen times more likely to experience rape or attempted rape in the first year of college.
- Childhood victims of prolonged sexual abuse nearly always develop feelings of worthlessness. Many become suicidal.[1]

Is it any wonder our nation is in trouble? We live on the edge of a volcano and can feel it rumbling just beneath the surface. I once wrote in my diary about this disturbing image:

> On the edge of a volcano
> I have lived for many years
> Now it seems the distant rumble's getting louder in my ears
> I have tried to walk away from broken pieces of my past
> But their edges tear my feet like shattered glass
> I have tried to push disturbing thoughts beyond the reach of man
> I have tried to burn my bridges but I've only burned my hand
> Pushing things under the carpet hoping that they'll go away
> But I know I'll lose my balance any day.[2]

No matter how "together" we look or how rich and famous we may become, the distant rumble troubles every one of us.

The loudest voices sometimes conceal the most broken spirits.

The angriest individuals sometimes are the most afraid.

The very quiet sometimes have much to say but remain silent because they still hear parents and teachers yelling at them to shut up.

I wish it were different in the church. Too often it's not.

In January 2013, author and teacher Lysa TerKeurst and I hosted a live webcast titled "Silencing Your Negative Inside Chatter." I wasn't quite sure what a "webcast" was, so Lysa patiently explained that we would sit on the platform of a church in North Carolina, her ministry's home base. We would deliver our teaching to a camera, and women from around the country could sign in on their computers and watch us live. Through Facebook and Twitter they also could ask questions for us to address on air. Women could watch the webcast for free, but they had to sign up ahead of time to get access. This would also tell us how many viewers had joined us. I had no idea how many to expect, but neither Lysa nor I anticipated the more than fifty thousand women who signed in that night and for the re-air the following day. The title had clearly struck a chord.

Women in general consider "negative inside chatter" a huge issue, but so do women who love Christ. Although we Christians voice our belief in the fierce love of God, internally we tear ourselves to shreds. Too often we allow the loud wail of what we feel to drown out the truth of what we believe.

When we are not secure in the truth, we place blame on all sorts of things for how we feel inside. Or at least we hold them responsible. Of all the issues we struggle with, why do you think this one—insecurity—feels so primal and so hard to eradicate? Perhaps it's because our security was the first thing to fall in the garden.

DESCENT FROM CONFIDENCE

Although we probably speak more of shame than of insecurity, insecurity opened the door to shame. Adam and Eve were the first to have to deal with this ugly invasion. They hid because they felt insecure and unsafe.

So she took some of the fruit and ate it. Then she gave some to her husband, who was with her, and he ate it, too. At that moment their eyes were opened, and they suddenly felt shame at their nakedness. So they sewed fig leaves together to cover themselves. (Genesis 3:6–7)

The enemy saw it all. He saw their descent from quiet confidence in the love and friendship of God to the gaping soul-wound that made them hide. His weapon worked quite well in the garden and continues to work equally well today.

So what are we to do about it?

Only one thing can help us. We must replace the lies we have believed for the truth of who God says we are.

Paul gets at the heart of the insecurity issue in the fifth chapter of Romans:

When we were utterly helpless, Christ came at just the right time and died for us sinners. Now, most people would not be willing to die for an upright person, though someone might perhaps be willing to die for a person who is especially good. But God showed his great love for us by sending Christ to die for us while we were still sinners. And since we have been made right in God's sight by the blood of Christ, he will certainly save us from God's condemnation. For since our friendship with God was restored by the death of his Son while we were still his enemies, we will certainly be saved through the life of his Son. So now we can rejoice in our wonderful new relationship with God because our Lord Jesus Christ has made us friends of God. (vv. 6–11)

I love so many things about this passage! I love that it acknowledges the truth about who we are without Christ—helpless sinners. Before we can embrace the good news of the love of God, we have to deal with the truth of who we are without Him. But since our culture considers that truth unpopular, too often we in the church downplay it. While I might wish that the church would set the standard for what becomes popular in culture, usually it goes the other way around. And in a similar way, unpopular things in our culture tend to become unpopular in our churches.

A friend of mine drew my attention to an article that appeared recently in his local paper. It carried the headline "Just in Time for Lent: A New Sense of Sin." The article reported how John Frohnmayer, the former director of the National Endowment for the Humanities, suggested replacing the old "seven deadly sins" with a modern list that he thinks better fits our culture. The old list, of course, never carried the authority of divine inspiration; it came from the pen of a fourth-century monastic. But I found Frohnmayer's rationale for "updating" the old list both fascinating and troubling.

While Frohnmayer admits the original sense of the word *sin* describes something that offends God, he contends that "sin, or whatever you want to call it, really is much more important if it offends society now than a higher power." Thus, for him, pride is healthy, envy is positive (because it inspires us to do better), and "without lust, the human race is toast."[3]

The arrogant conclusion of his reasoning is basically, "Sorry, God, but You're *so* out-of-date."

To our own hurt, we frequently allow the popular voices of our culture to exert undue influence over us. Therefore, since love is "in" but sin is "out," in our churches we talk incessantly of a God of love but hardly ever mention how much He hates sin.

Yes, *hates*.

The Word of God doesn't shy away from that. It even publishes a list of the top seven things God hates the most (Proverbs 6:16–19).

The issue goes far beyond redefining sin, of course. We allow "popular" cultural voices to tell us how to look, what kind of clothes to wear, what career paths our children should choose, where we should live, and on and on.

Let me ask: Do you want to enjoy a quiet confidence in God? If so, then you must resist the ridiculous nonsense that the mass media spoon-feeds you and me every day.

You do *not* have to be a size 8 to be happy.

You do *not* need the latest styles to have value.

Your children do *not* have to make straight As for you to be a good parent.

In Romans 5, Paul stated the simple truth that before we even knew about the love of God, Christ died for us. He did so, not because we had earned it, but because He loves us.

We are made right with God, not because we follow a list of "Twenty Things to Do to Be a Godly Woman," but because of the shed blood of Christ.

Does that sound overly simple? Maybe. But somehow, we miss the statement's profound depth, and therefore we struggle with its truth. Think about it. When you wake up in the morning, do you think, *Oh, I am so glad that God loves me simply because Jesus died for me! This is going to make my day so much easier!*

If you're like me, that's probably not your first thought.

When you have a bad day and you yell at your kids or call your husband a name not found in the New Testament, is your first thought, *Well, I blew it there, but thanks be to God that His love is not based on my behavior but on the finished work of Christ?*

Again, probably not.

Most of us struggle with this. In every relationship we have on earth—from our parents and siblings, to schoolmates, to college friends, to coworkers, to our spouses and children—we receive input as to how well or poorly we have performed. Every criticism feeds the insecurity we already feel. I know that to be true in my own life. If I've spoken to two thousand women who received my message warmly but one woman tells me that she expected something a bit deeper—that's all I hear and the storm of insecurity begins.

You should have spent more time preparing!
You're just not a good teacher!
Maybe you shouldn't do this anymore.

It's ridiculous that one comment from someone can send me off the cliff of a deep, quiet confidence in God into an abyss of self-doubt. One unkind or even mildly critical comment from one mother to another can have the most confident of moms believing she's a failure. Because that is the harsh ongoing reality of life on this earth, it is such a struggle to freely receive God's love and mercy. The very fact that God requires nothing of us except faith and trust goes against our fragile hearts. Our world survives by comparison. It's how we judge.

Is this phone better than that phone?
Is this skirt a more flattering shape than that skirt?
Do her children behave better than my children?

On and on the internal dialogue goes, and when we believe that we fall short, the waves of insecurity rise up.

But believing is a choice. If you wait until you "feel" worthy of the love of God, then you will die waiting. We must receive by faith the truth that Christ has made us worthy.

THE EXAMPLE OF ABRAHAM

Abraham *believed* God, and the Lord counted his faith as righteousness. The Bible doesn't say God declared Abraham righteous because the man got a lot of things right. Listen to what Paul says about Abraham, the great father of our faith:

> For if Abraham was justified by works, he has something to boast about, but not before God. For what does the Scripture say? "Abraham believed God, and it was counted to him as righteousness." (Romans 4:2–3 ESV)

A little later in the passage, Paul unpacks that truth even further (he also includes us in the picture).

Abraham never wavered in believing God's promise. In fact, his faith grew stronger, and in this he brought glory to God. He was fully convinced that God is able to do whatever he promises. And because of Abraham's faith, God counted him as righteous. And when God counted him as righteous, it wasn't just for Abraham's benefit. It was recorded for our benefit, too, assuring us that God will also count us as righteous if we believe in him, the one who raised Jesus our Lord from the dead. He was handed over to die because of our sins, and he was raised to life to make us right with God. (Romans 4:20–25)

Paul starts right where the breach began, where insecurity started to run in our veins. And he takes us to where we are in Christ—if we will just believe.

Yes, Adam's one sin brings condemnation for everyone, but Christ's one act of righteousness brings a right relationship with God and new life for everyone. Because one person disobeyed God, many became sinners. But because one other person obeyed God, many will be made righteous. (Romans 5:18–19)

If you're thinking, *Sheila, this sounds more like a sermon on justification by faith than a chapter addressing my insecurity*, then I'd like to ask you to reframe our discussion. Think of it this way: while insecurity tells us we are *not* right, the righteousness of Christ *makes* us right.

That is a biblical fact . . . even though we don't always feel it. Abraham had utter confidence that God would do what *He* had promised, not what Abraham had promised. In fact, one of the most beautiful encounters that ever took place between God and Abraham made this fact crystal clear—and it didn't happen at a time of great faith, but at a time of deep questioning.

Abram (God had not yet changed his name to Abraham) wanted a son more than anything. In those days, a man with no son would pass all his wealth to a trusted servant (Genesis 15). With brutal honesty, Abram told God that he didn't understand what He meant by calling him "blessed," since he had no son. God did not rebuke Abram for insolence. Instead, He walked him outside the tent under the great vault of the heavens, directing his attention up toward the Milky Way. Can you imagine how amazing those skies must have looked, with not a single electric light burning in the whole world?

God asked Abram if he could count the stars.

Abram knew he couldn't. No one could.

Then God told him that his offspring would outnumber the stars.

And though he had no children at all, Abram believed God.

We read, "And Abram believed the LORD, and the LORD counted him as righteous because of his faith" (Genesis 15:6).

Now, if the story ended there, you might be tempted to say, "Well, you have to give it to old Abram. He really did have a bucket load of faith." But we need to read on through the next couple of verses.

> Then the LORD told him, "I am the LORD who brought you out of Ur of the Chaldeans to give you this land as your possession." But Abram replied, "O Sovereign LORD, how can I be sure that I will actually possess it?" (vv. 7–8)

Perhaps your spiritual life is one of your greatest areas of insecurity. You question the level of your faith, constantly comparing yourself to others who grasp the promises of God. If that's you, you're like Abram. He believed God, but he still questioned how it was possible. The reason he questioned God and the reason we do, too, is because we know ourselves. We know our limitations and the flawed frailty of our humanity. But God was about to show Abram that the reason he can stand in confidence had absolutely nothing to do with himself.

God chose this moment in history to do the most shocking and marvelous thing. It will seem a little strange at first, but hang in there. It is *very* good news for us!

The Lord told him, "Bring me a three-year-old heifer, a three-year-old female goat, a three-year-old ram, a turtledove, and a young pigeon." So Abram presented all these to him and killed them. Then he cut each animal down the middle and laid the halves side by side. . . .

As the sun was going down, Abram fell into a deep sleep, and a terrifying darkness came down over him. . . .

After the sun went down and darkness fell, Abram saw a smoking firepot and a flaming torch pass between the halves of the carcasses. So the Lord made a covenant with Abram that day. (Genesis 15:9–10, 12, 17–18)

If you're at all like me, you probably have a visceral reaction against stories like this one. I have zero desire to kill a goat and cut it down the middle! I still twitch when Christian and I pull the dried-out wishbone from our Christmas turkey to see who gets the big half.

The most common Hebrew word for "making" a covenant is *karat*, or to "cut" a covenant. In Abram's time, several types of covenants existed, including a covenant formalized by eating together (covenants of "bread" or "salt"). But the most binding of all covenants was the covenant of blood, formalized by passing through the divided halves of sacrificed animals.

God made exactly this kind of covenant with Abram. The smoking firepot and flaming torch symbolized God's presence. But the Lord altered one part of the usual ceremony. Normally, both parties passed through the animal carcasses together; but in this covenant with Abram, God alone passed through the bloody sacrifices. Commentator David Baron explains why:

According to the ancient Eastern manner of making a covenant, both the contracting parties passed through the divided pieces of the slain animals, thus symbolically attesting that they pledged their very lives to the fulfillment of the engagement they made (see Jer. 34:18, 19). Now in Genesis 15, God alone, whose presence was symbolized by the smoking furnace and lamp of fire, passed through the midst of the pieces of the slain animals, while Abram was simply a spectator of this wonderful exhibition of God's free grace.[4]

Do you see the beauty and grace at work here? Do you see why we can choose to shift our battered hearts from feelings of insecurity to a place of confidence? In the typical expression of this covenant, both parties passed through the blood, in effect saying, "May I be torn in two if I break this agreement!" But since Abram had no part in making the covenant, he also could do nothing to cancel it. The fulfillment of the covenant depended solely upon God.

It's the same with you and me. We contribute *nothing* to our salvation. What Christ did on the cross brought to completion what we saw God doing for Abram. It's as if He says to you and me,

"This is not about you; it's all about Me."

"You will fail Me, but I will never fail you."

"You will fall down and get back up, but I will always be standing right here for you."

All we can do—all God asks us to do—is put our trust in Jesus. God will keep His covenant promise to save us, for Jesus' sake.

THE KEY ROLE OF TRUST

So then, how does all of this help us with our insecurity? How can it give us the ability to move to a place of absolute confidence in God? I believe it all begins with a small, huge word: *TRUST*. Trust to me feels like giving love feet. We show God how much we love Him by intentionally dragging our feelings of insecurity in line with who God's Word says we are and acting on that truth rather than the familiar lies we have believed.

Our culture waters down and generalizes the term *love* to refer to anything from ice cream to your children, but not so with the term *trust*. While you might still love someone who has deeply hurt you, you may not be able to trust him or her.

Of course, we exercise different levels of trust in various people and institutions—we might trust our auto mechanic with our car, trust our banker with our money, and trust our doctor with our health—but the essential meaning of the term remains the same. To trust someone means to place confidence in him or her to follow through on some expressed commitment.

The greatest challenge to exchanging our insecurity for confidence in God is that we still live on this planet. Check your zip code. If you don't see "Pearly Gates," then you're still down here. You're still right in the middle of a cosmic war zone. And that means people will wound you, people will fail you, people will let you down.

But not God!

God will never fail you. Only He is worthy of your complete trust. In Him alone you can place 100 percent confidence.

I am still learning this lesson. After forty years of walking with God, insecurity still rears its devilish head. It did so again just last week.

In 2013 Women of Faith made some changes. We brought in some amazing women as new speakers. In January of that year we gathered for a retreat to enable us to get to know each other a bit, share our hearts, and pray for each other. I had a ridiculously busy schedule leading up to the retreat, and when I get really tired, I let my God-guard down.

We held the retreat at a site about two hours from Dallas, so I decided to drive down by myself instead of meeting everyone at our offices and taking the bus. I stopped halfway there to fill up with gas and read a text from our vice president of Creative. He had a simple request: "Will you lead off the first session in the afternoon and just bring everyone up to speed on the history of Women of Faith?" He hadn't asked me to explain rocket science. He'd made a simple, commonsense request. But do you know what took place inside of me?

I can't do that!

I can't stand up in front of these amazing women and speak!

I don't think I belong anymore!

I've passed my shelf life!

I started dying internally . . . and the enemy loved it. I quickly found a quiet spot on the road, away from people and traffic, and had a heart-to-heart with my Father: "Well, here I am again, Lord! I'm so sorry, but I feel over-whelmed. Despite everything You've done in my life, I still feel like the little girl clinging onto her blouse. I still feel it would be a relief to everyone if I didn't show up. I still hear people talking about me in little groups."

For some time, I sat there in my Father's presence. Then I put on my new CD from Hillsong Australia, and waited for track 2: "Beneath the Waters I Will Rise."

> I rise as you are risen; declare your rule and reign
> My life, confess Your Lordship and glorify your name
> Your word, it stands eternal; your kingdom knows no end
> Your praise goes on forever and on and on again
> No power can stand against you
> No curse assault your throne
> No one can steal your glory, for it is yours alone
> I stand to sing your praises
> I stand to testify, for I was dead in my sin
> Now I *rise*

More often than not, for me, trusting means consciously dragging my will into line with the will of God, no matter what I feel. I stand on what is true and not on what *feels* true.

Will I get it wrong sometimes? Yes!

Will some people criticize or misunderstand me? Yes!

Will I occasionally get left out of things I wish I were a part of? Yes!

But still I stand.

DEPEND ON HIM

A line from the book of Proverbs beautifully sums up my bottom line on insecurity.

Trust in the LORD with all your heart;
   do not depend on your own understanding.
Seek his will in all you do,
   and he will show you which path to take.

Don't be impressed with your own wisdom.
   Instead, fear the LORD and turn away from evil.
Then you will have healing for your body
   and strength for your bones. (3:5–8)

When insecurity rears its ugly head (and it will), we can say, "Well, *you* might not choose me, *you* might not value me, *you* might not even want me around . . . but *God* does!" Remember this verse; try to commit it to memory:

"Now you are my friends, since I have told you everything the Father told me. You didn't choose me. I chose you." (John 15:15–16)

Do you find it hard to memorize verses (and, sister, I am right there with you!)? If so, just remember the final part, for they are Christ's words to you:

"You didn't choose Me. I chose you."
"You didn't choose Me. I chose you."
"You didn't choose Me. I chose you."
"You didn't choose Me. I CHOSE YOU."

And because He chose you, the same unconditional covenant that swept Abram into God's eternal family also sweeps you there. Just as God passed through the sacrifices alone, so did Jesus pass through Calvary alone. He chose you and *you are His*.

Forever!

STANDING THROUGH YOUR STORM

Some emotions are easier to provide space for than others because they are produced by circumstances that for most of us are rare moments as opposed to a continuous reality. We may face despair for a season, but it will pass. We may be heartbroken by an unexpected loss or tragedy, but the pain makes sense because of what we are walking through. The challenge with insecurity is that it is so pervasive. We are presented with a hundred opportunities to go there every day. So how do we stand?

1. The next time insecurity comes knocking, run to His Word. Remember that God's love for you has nothing to do with your performance. I'll let you into a strange little secret of mine. In my bathroom, which is where I go first most mornings, I have three little rubber ducks, the kind a child would play with in his or her bath. I have two going in one direction and one going the other way. It's my daily reminder that I will never have all my ducks in a row, and that's okay.

2. Remember, too, the glorious news that God chose you; you didn't choose Him. He still chooses you, on the days when you feel as if you got it all right and on the days when you feel as if you got it all wrong.

3. Hear Him say one final thing:

> "Never will I leave you;
>> Never will I forsake you."
> So we say with confidence,
> "The Lord is my helper; I will not be afraid.
> What can mere mortals do to me?" (Hebrews 13:5, 6 NIV)

CHAPTER EIGHT

A New Dawn Breaks

From Insignificance to Courage

*Either the well was very deep, or she fell very slowly, for she had
plenty of time as she went down to look about her and to wonder
what was going to happen next.*

—Lewis Carroll, *Alice's Adventures in Wonderland*

*Be strong and courageous; don't be terrified or afraid of them. For
it is the Lord your God who goes with you; He will not leave you or
forsake you.*

—Deuteronomy 31:6 (hcsb)

In the late eighties, early nineties, I hosted my own thirty-minute daily
talk show, *Heart to Heart.* I met so many amazing people, people who
didn't always get the miracle they prayed for and yet still loved God.
My producer, Cheryl, and I looked for stories that showed the mystery of
God's presence when nothing else made sense. We freed ourselves of the
restraint that every story had to end well, because not every story does. I
used the plumb line of my passionate belief that when your real story, *all* of
it, encounters a real God, anything is possible. It just might not look like
you expected it to.

Many people left an indelible imprint on my heart.

- *Charlie Wedemeyer*, a high school teacher and football coach whose faith shone even through the ravages of Lou Gehrig's disease.
- *Noah Snider*, who fell quickly from a normal life to a life on the streets, becoming both homeless and nameless.
- *Pilot Eugene "Red" McDaniel*, shot down over North Vietnamese territory and held in the "Hanoi Hilton" (the name given to the worst prison during the Vietnam War) for six years.

Each of these men talked about struggling with their faith, about wrestling with God in the darkest places imaginable, and yet finding Him faithful. But one little woman captivated me the most.

From the first moment I met Huldah Buntain, she felt like family to me. Even as she sat down on the set and crossed her hands on her lap, I remember thinking, *I feel like I know you.* I had read her book, *Treasures in Heaven*, the night before we met; but then, I always read my guests' books. There was something more about Huldah.

Something about Huldah . . .

I loved her transparent, even brutal honesty. She and her husband, Mark, had served as missionaries in India for more than thirty years. Perhaps my heart connected so deeply with Huldah because she had lived my dream.

As a young woman I believed that God had called me to India. I went to seminary in London to prepare for that mission. I bought a map of India and put it up on the wall in my college dorm room. Every morning and evening as I prayed for the women of India, tears poured down my face. I never experienced that kind of prayer burden before or since.

But when I graduated from seminary, God redirected my steps to work in Europe with Youth for Christ. I find it ironic that now I have set foot on almost every country on the planet—except India.

India may have been *my* dream, but it certainly wasn't Huldah's. She didn't want to be a missionary. She didn't even want to be a pastor's wife. In *Treasures in Heaven*, she wrote,

"God," I prayed silently, *"I have lived most of my life sacrificially. I like nice things. Please don't ask me to be a preacher's wife. I'll do anything You ask, but please God, not the ministry."*[1]

I laughed out loud when I read that bit. I wonder how many of us have prayed that kind of prayer. The "I'll do this and this and this, but not that" kind of prayer. Do you think that somehow, deep inside, we know God is calling us, and we're just trying to cut Him off at the pass? If so, the strategy has never worked for me.

And it certainly didn't work for Huldah.

She and Mark fell in love and married and, in 1954, secured passage on a ship to begin their work in India. I say "ship," but don't think "cruise ship." Their vessel had nothing in common with Disney's Big Red Boat or the Holland American Cruise Line. They stayed in a dark cubicle in the hull of the ship. As Mark quipped, "There's first class, second class, third class, and missionary class." He saw it as funny, but Huldah was not amused.

Mark felt excited about his calling to a land teeming with millions who had never heard the gospel of Christ, but Huldah had no heart for India. They had made an initial commitment for one year, and she prayed fervently that after twelve months had passed they could return to America, particularly after the birth of their daughter. She didn't think they could safely raise a child in a country overrun by poverty and disease, and, like most of us with a young child, she wanted her family nearby.

At the end of that year, however, Mark knew God had called him to give his life to the people of India. Huldah remained unconvinced but loyal: "God did not call me to India, but He did call me to be Mark's wife."

As I listened to Huldah talk about the realities of establishing a church in a foreign country, of fighting government restrictions that made no sense, of running out of supplies in the face of overwhelming need, I had to take off my rose-colored glasses. As a teenager I had a very romantic, unrealistic idea of life on the mission field. I imagined it would go something like this:

I would disembark my ship and step onto Indian soil and immediately children would surround me, welcoming me to their country. Within a year hundreds would surrender their lives to Christ through my ministry and flock to the Bible studies I held in my little hut.

Naïve and clueless.

Huldah discovered (and lived) a very different scene. It soon became clear that people the world over are remarkably the same. The kinds of problems that plague the local church in Pittsburgh, also bedevil the one in Calcutta. Night after night, Mark came home discouraged and worn down from disputes with the deacon board. It all made Huldah furious. She described her pillow as "a launching pad for my vengeful thoughts."

Huldah could see, though, that love for the Indian people ran in Mark's veins, and over time she began to share it. They fed the hungry, cared for the sick, and built up the body of Christ. Eventually they helped establish a large inner-city church in Calcutta, as well as a nationally recognized hospital.

But they had to weather storms they never anticipated, including the ongoing thundercloud of Mark's health. Twice he had to return to the United States for back surgeries and to get the care required for recovery. The last storm packed too much of a punch to overcome. Mark suffered a massive cerebral hemorrhage and did not survive a surgery designed to release pressure on his brain.

His death devastated Huldah. I imagine that when you share the kind of life they shared, without the comforts of home, the bond between you either gets strained to a breaking point or becomes unbreakable. For Mark and Huldah, it was the latter.

He had expressed his desire to be buried in India, and with the government's permission, his casket was lowered into the foundations of a new sanctuary under construction. He lived to serve God and the people of India, and his bones rest perpetually where his heart beat strongest. Thousands attended his funeral, and as Huldah watched them march past his casket with tears running down their faces, she finally realized that now, she could go home.

At long last, she felt free to return to America to family and friends.

And then God spoke.

Have you noticed how often God does that? You have your plan all in place, your ducks in a row . . . and suddenly, God speaks. Huldah wrote, "I found myself permeated with the same divine call that had driven Mark. I sensed my own ordination to continue the work among the people of the land I had grown to love."

She still serves in India today. Last year I received an unexpected gift. Huldah returned home for a brief stateside visit, recorded a message on a friend's iPhone, and sent it to me. Twenty-three years had elapsed since I had interviewed her. I felt deeply touched that she remembered me.

If you go to the website of the Mercy Hospital in Calcutta, India, you'll see their logo in the shape of two hands cupped, as if to pour out. Huldah explained why:

> Every morning on the edge of the Ganges, Indians wade into the ancient river, cup a handful of water in their hands, and pour it out to symbolize a self-sacrificial offering. In India, the imagery of this action has come to represent selfless giving and commitment to a noble cause. We use it in our logo to communicate our dedication to pouring out ourselves to self-lessly serve the people of Calcutta, especially the underprivileged.[2]

If you had sat down with Huldah in her early years and told her of the decades she would spend in India, that Mark would die there, but that she would choose to continue the work, she would have bluntly told you, "You're crazy." She wanted to live a simple life, be comfortable, and raise her family, not rock the boat.

But God had much bigger plans. When Huldah said yes to Mark, she had no way of knowing that she was saying yes to God as well. That first step of faith, marrying a man in ministry, was just the first in a long journey that would transform this little woman from someone who wanted to remain insignificant on the world's stage to the woman of courage who still serves in India today. Just one step can change the course of a life.

I have a strong feeling as I write today that He has much bigger plans for each one of His daughters, if only we would trust Him. Perhaps you, like me, are acutely aware of what you can't do. When I graduated from high school, one of my friends wrote in my yearbook: "Most likely to stay at home." She saw it as tongue-in-cheek humor, but she hit the nail on the head. My life felt far too insignificant to ever do anything great for God. Courage was for other people less damaged than I was. Even now new challenges intimidate me. I can always suggest twenty other women I believe have far better qualifications for the job.

But I am becoming a big fan of the word *courage*. As I've walked with God for more than forty years now, I see a difference between godly courage and foolhardiness, between human strength and utter dependence on the One who gives me strength. I believe God is calling all of us to a life of significance for His kingdom. Hollywood would have no idea what to do with such a story, because it's all about Jesus and not about us. So perhaps before we can understand God's dream, we need to debunk a few myths of our own.

OUR DREAMS . . . AND HIS

As a young girl were you more of the "one day my prince will come and we will live happily ever after" kind of child who saw her significance in the beauty and strength of her family, or did you want to storm the castle yourself? Unless someone crushed your ability to dream at a very early age, most of us imagine doing something of significance with our lives. We might not change the world, but we might change our part of it.

At sixteen I wanted to be a nurse—until I visited our pastor's wife in the hospital after nose surgery. It must have been time to change her dressing, because the next thing I knew, I woke up in the bed next to her. My motto became, "All blood should be kept in the body whenever possible!"

You may have dreamed about getting married and starting a family, or following a chosen career path, or perhaps you decided to let your life unfold as you went along. But each of these dreams has an inherent flaw. Even if you do marry the finest man who ever walked the earth, have super-children, and climb to the top of the ladder in your chosen field, still your dream will lack *something*. So long as we live on this earth, our human dreams will never live up to their preview.

Not so with God's dreams. They concern ordinary women like you and me, daring to believe that anything is possible because He lives in and through us. As George Eliot wrote, "It is never too late to be what you might have been."

In 2013 a news bulletin shocked the world: "Pope Benedict says he will resign, as he no longer has the strength to fulfill the duties of his office." I don't know much about Roman Catholic history, but I know he is the first pope to resign since the Middle Ages, more than six hundred years ago. That is a *huge* deal. It had to take a lot of courage to do that. I can't imagine the internal process that must have taken place. I'm sure many voices insisted, "You can't *do* that!" But he clearly believed he had served his time and now must step down, no matter what others thought or how they responded.

If, then, we were to draw a broader point from a narrow story, we might conclude that saying yes to God sometimes requires saying no to others.

It's not as easy as it sounds.

Many women have told me about the frustration of living what others have dreamed for them rather than heading where they wanted their own lives to go. Someone once asked me, "If you could talk now as a grown woman to your sixteen-year-old self, what would you tell her?"

"Run!" I replied.

Not really, but I would tell her not to worry so much about what others think of her, because there's a good chance they never think about her at all! And even if they did entertain unflattering thoughts of her, I would declare that God adores her and that as many times as she falls down, He will help her up again.

If you could sit down with the sixteen-year-old version of yourself and ask her the following questions, how do you think she would respond?

- Do you feel as if your voice is heard?
- Do your dreams matter to those who love you?

- Will you get to choose the career path you want?
- Do you believe that others take you seriously?
- Do you want to do something big for God?

I wonder what she would say—that younger version of yourself? Perhaps you married very young, and as baby after baby came along, any other dream got lost beneath a growing mountain of diapers and dirty dishes. Don't get me wrong; I think being a mom is glorious. I think it's one of the most challenging, fulfilling, frustrating callings that God ever places on us.

But I want to address here the lies that the enemy might be whispering right now in the depths of your heart, no matter where you spend your days, whether in the corner office or the corner store.

> *Is this all you're going to do with your life?*
> *You used to be a dreamer, but not anymore.*
> *Even as you fall into bed after one more exhausting day,*
> *don't you see that you did nothing of real significance?*
> *Your life makes no difference at all.*

Those lies all bear the same return address: hell.

Your life *matters* to God. We live in a culture that glamorizes fame and gives worth to things that have no lasting value. I often wonder if the mom who tucks a prayer into every piece of laundry she folds realizes—even begins to conceive of—the difference she is making. So, too, with a female executive in a successful business when she bathes each transaction in prayer and looks for those "God moments" when she must speak up.

I think every Christian woman should receive some kind of covert-operator's badge to remind us that we actually serve another King. Our King looks not for the one with the most impressive skill set, but the one with the heart of a servant who knows when to stand and serve. Who in this world would have chosen a twelve-year-old girl from an obscure village of less than two thousand people to be the mother of Christ? Those in Nazareth who knew Mary would have seen her as a sweet girl, who would get married, have a family, and settle down to a quiet life. God looked at Mary's heart and took her on a profound journey from insignificance to courage. The world might look at you and place no value on who you are, but that is its mistake. As Paul wrote to the church in Corinth,

> Brothers, consider your calling: Not many are wise from a human per-
> spective, not many powerful, not many of noble birth. Instead, God has
> chosen what is foolish in the world to shame the wise, and God has
> chosen what is weak in the world to shame the strong. God has chosen
> what is insignificant and despised in the world—what is viewed as noth-
> ing—to bring to nothing what is viewed as something. (1 Corinthians
> 1:26–28 HCSB)

Paul uses pretty strong language here, not to shame the Corinthians, but to wake them up a little. He wants to remind them of their backgrounds, who they are in Christ, and how great God is. The word translated *insignifi-cant* denotes the opposite of *noble*; it means "of no great importance in this world." The word rendered *despised* means more than simply looked down upon, but something closer to "branded with contempt." The same word in Luke 23:11 describes how Herod treated Christ: "And Herod with his soldiers treated him with contempt and mocked him" (ESV).

Paul made it clear that what has little significance in the world has monumental significance to God. It seems to be a bit of a glorious, divine joke that God uses the least likely people to do mighty things for Him. He's done that for millennia—and still does. You and I are the proof.

One of my pet projects is to try and debunk the myth of the platform or the stage. We think that if someone walks into a pulpit or onto a stage, nicely dressed, with a Bible in one hand and a mic in the other, she is more special, more chosen, more "anointed" than the woman who slips into her seat with her hair pulled back into a banana clip and with spit-up on her shoulder.

No!

True significance in the kingdom of God *never* comes from talent or charisma, but from love—and true love takes courage.

You might feel tempted to think, *Thanks, but this information is too little, too late.* While I don't want to ruin the punch line of the gospel, I must tell you that the radical, great, hilarious news of the kingdom of God is that it is *never* too late to step up and say, "Okay, I'm in!"

Okay, okay, I hear your objection. "I can hardly keep the laundry up-to-date," you say, "and you want me to go out and change the world? I'm changing a diaper, and that's about all I can handle!"

I believe with everything in me that God is raising up an army of ragtag women of all shapes and sizes around the world who have grown tired of listening to the enemy's no and are ready to believe God's yes!

I'm not for a moment suggesting you ditch your life and go out and conquer North Dakota for Jesus. I just want you to remember that you—yes, you—are part of this amazing thing that God is doing on the earth. I have followed Christ for forty-five years, but I've never felt such a shift in the spiritual atmosphere as I do today. God is on the move—and I want to be part of what He is doing.

And I want you to be a part of it as well.

It's the reason why I wrote this book, when I had plenty of other things pulling at my time and attention. This is *important.*

I believe with everything in me that God is raising up an army of ragtag women of all shapes and sizes around the world who have grown tired of listening to the enemy's no and are ready to believe God's yes!

Am I talking about revival? Well, yes. But perhaps in a way none of us have ever seen it. I've often heard people talk about revival in America, but I've never myself had a deep sense of its imminence. In my twenties and thirties, I received many invitations to sing at "revival meetings," but the only thing I ever saw revived appeared to be last week's green bean casserole.

As a seminary student, I studied many of the great revivals of Christian history. I studied the great Welsh revival of 1904. The revival storm that hit the hills and valleys of Wales that year soon became a hurricane whose divine winds blew around the world. Visitors from around the globe came to visit and, deeply impacted, took home the still-burning flames.

Another powerful revival shook the Hebrides Islands of my homeland, Scotland, in 1949. Duncan Campbell, who received an invitation to preach there, described it like this:

> God was beginning to move, the heavens were opening, we were there on our faces before God. Three o'clock in the morning came, and GOD SWEPT IN. About a dozen men and women lay prostrate on the floor, speechless. Something had happened; we knew that the forces of darkness were going to be driven back, and men were going to be delivered. We left the cottage at 3 am to discover men and women seeking God. I walked along a country road, and found three men on their faces, crying to God for mercy. There was a light in every home, no one seemed to think of sleep.[3]

These great revivals, and others like them, were birthed out of the fervent, committed prayers of believers who would not let go of God until He answered them. I love that historians have traced the beginning of the Scottish revival back to two sisters, Peggy and Christine Smith, at the time ages eighty-two and eighty-four. They had prayed constantly for revival.

As I ponder many of the revivals that have visited the earth, it seems to me as though God, for a moment, opened the heavens, lavishly poured out His Spirit, and then moved on.

I don't know if we will see that kind of revival in our day, but I am praying for it daily. But I do know that God is in the business of reviving ordinary women like you and me, and teaching us how to live with courage and passion. I saw that with Huldah. I saw that with my mother, who at sixty-five knew it was too late for her to be a teacher—until someone challenged her to teach a Bible study in her home.

Scripture overflows with stories of men and women who felt insignificant until they found themselves at a spiritual crossroads.

Those moments can change a life.

If God wills, they can change a nation.

AN "ESTHER MOMENT"

The Old Testament story of Esther clearly illustrates the transformation from insignificance to courage. I think Esther embodies the profound statement made by Viktor Frankl: "When we are no longer able to change a situation, we are challenged to change ourselves."

I find the book of Esther remarkable in many ways. For one thing, it is one of only two books in the Bible named after a woman (Ruth is the other). Second, although the book never once mentions God, it clearly portrays Him as the hero.

Esther's story seems so compelling to me because no one asked her if she wanted to step up and have courage; she simply got rounded up in a cattle call at the whim of the most powerful man on the planet at that time, King Xerxes.

Four years before, his beautiful wife, Queen Vashti, had refused to be treated like a performing poodle in front of some drunken guests, and his advisors counseled him to divorce her. He did. But eventually he got lonely, and so his advisors (get some new counselors, dude!) came up with an obscene plan. They suggested sending men out to scour his vast empire to gather all the young, beautiful, virgin teenage girls. That's where we meet Esther; she got caught in that net. She didn't volunteer and nobody consulted her. She got conscripted on two counts:

1. She was beautiful.
2. She was a virgin.

Just try to imagine her situation. She was sitting down to a quiet meal one night when a soldier banged at the door. When her uncle answered, the soldier dragged her away. Imagine how Mordecai must have felt. He had stepped up to care for Esther after her mother and father died. He raised her as his own, and now someone was dragging away his lovely young niece, and there was nothing he could do about it. Afraid for her life, he instructed her to keep her Jewishness a secret.

Royal handlers soaked and scrubbed the girls and marinated them in perfumed oils for an entire year before they were presented to the king to see which one he found the most succulent—like a Christmas goose on a platter. Well, Esther "won" the Miss Persia contest hands down, and King Xerxes made her his new queen.

We probably would call it a marriage in name only. He called for Esther when he wanted to sleep with her, but he had many concubines. Weeks would go by without Esther getting a call from her husband. In many ways, she had both everything and nothing. She was a Jewess living as a pagan queen. She had a husband but no real marital intimacy. She had a lot of shiny stuff but not her husband's heart. She had been given a title of significance but a life empty of meaning.

Into that bleak, opulent picture the Lord gave her the opportunity to step from insignificance to courage. She was about to rediscover what really belonged to her.

Throughout biblical history, Satan had repeatedly plotted to destroy God's people, and under King Xerxes' rule, once again his plans slithered to the surface. Haman, the king's chief advisor, was a profoundly arrogant and evil man who required that everyone who walked past him should bow in reverence. Mordecai refused to do this, saying that only God is worthy of worship. This infuriated Haman, and when he discovered that Mordecai was a Jew, he hatched a plot to have every Jewish man, woman, and child slaughtered. He presented his plan to the king under the manufactured threat that the Jewish people were becoming rebellious and a menace to the throne.

Just like Satan, Haman thought he had every angle covered. He realized that the king might consider the tax revenue he would lose from this mass execution, so he offered to pay the king the equivalent of five million dollars of his own money. This was Haman's thirty pieces of silver.

Xerxes believed Haman and issued a decree that every Jew was to be executed. It's interesting to note that the decree was sent out on Passover, the day when all Jews celebrated their deliverance from Egypt. Once more it seemed as if the fate of God's people was sealed.

When Mordecai found out about it, he sent a message to Esther, asking her to speak to the king and beg for the lives of her people.

To understand the gravity of the requested intervention, we need to remember that *no one* could enter the king's presence without being summoned. To come unbidden invited the death penalty—and Xerxes had not sent for Esther in a month. I love what Carolyn James wrote: "Her first battle—even tougher than facing Xerxes—was to face and overcome herself."[4]

Mordecai's request horrified Esther. Did he have any idea what a disaster such a forced encounter might prompt? She fired a message back to her cousin and guardian, reminding him of what could happen to her if she entered the king's presence without a royal summons. Mordecai's response sounded like something you'd hear from a grizzled old prophet:

> Don't think for a moment that because you're in the palace you will escape when all the other Jews are killed. If you keep quiet at a time like this, deliverance and relief for the Jews will arise from some other place, but you and your relatives will die. Who knows if perhaps you were made queen for just such a time as this? (Esther 4:13–14)

Mordecai's reply convinced Esther to act. He made three profound points that overcame her fear and hesitancy:

1. You can't hide who you really are; truth always outs itself eventually, and when it does, you will die too.
2. God has promised to save His people, and He will keep His promise, with or without your help.
3. Esther, stand up. Maybe you became queen, at exactly this time, for exactly this emergency.

We, too, live in a world where the mention of the name of God is becoming more and more rare, even though we see His footprints everywhere. So how can Mordecai's words help us today?

First, human power—from the White House to the Kremlin to the most evil dictators—may seem like a big deal, but in the end it has no power ultimately to save anybody: "No king is saved by the size of his army; no warrior escapes by his great strength. A horse is a vain hope for deliverance; despite all its great strength it cannot save" (Psalm 33:16–17 NIV). God makes it clear that kind of "power" is insignificant.

Second, we live by the promises of God: "For no matter how many promises God has made, they are 'Yes' in Christ" (2 Corinthians 1:20 NIV). The psalmist depended on God's promise, and so he continued, "But the eyes of the LORD are on those who fear him, on those whose hope is in his unfailing love, to deliver them from death and keep them alive in famine" (Psalm 33:18–19 NIV). Our courage builds when we meditate on God's promises.

Third, to suppose that *I* might be alive at exactly *this* point in time and at exactly *this* place on earth in order to play a specific role specifically assigned to *me* by the King of the universe, who knows the end from the beginning—well, that takes courage from something generic and universal to something particular, individual, and beautiful.

Esther meditated on these things and then went to work. She fasted and prayed, asking all the Jewish people to join her. I *love* that. If you want to have courage like Esther, then you had better have a confidant like Mordecai! Even the bravest of souls need godly friends to help them find courage at fearsome times. Although Esther was about to display godly courage that came from the Lord, she saw it first modeled by her cousin. Just as Christ knelt in the Garden of Gethsemane on the night He was betrayed, so Esther knelt and prayed to her God. And after strengthening herself, she felt ready. She would walk with eyes wide open into whatever God allowed.

"And then," she said, "though it is against the law, I will go in to see the king. If I must die, I must die" (Esther 4:16).

This wasn't some triumphalistic, "I've got God in my pocket and I can work miracles." No, this was a humble servant of God convinced that God had called her to something terribly difficult at one of the greatest crossroads of her life. She found the courage to leave the outcome to God.

When Esther approached the king, she found favor with him and he welcomed her into his presence. She explained to her husband that Haman had basically sold her people for slaughter. The king reversed the decree against God's people and instead Haman was hung on the very gallows that he had constructed to kill Mordecai. Not only that, King Xerxes allowed Mordecai to write a new decree protecting the Jewish people, and the king sealed it with his own ring, a decree that could not be revoked. Pretty amazing story!

So what about us? I'm pretty sure I'm a bit long in the tooth to be rounded up for the Miss America pageant. No, we have a far greater calling: "And who knows whether you have not come to the kingdom for such a time as this?" (Esther 4:14 ESV).

Our own "Esther moments" will come, when the Lord will ask us to step out of what seems to be a place of insignificance and instead stand with courage for the King and His kingdom.

STANDING THROUGH YOUR STORM

I love Esther's story. I imagine her sitting around a fire later in life, talking about what God did. Who but God could be in control of a teenage girl, ripped out of her home and dragged off to be prepared and presented on a platter to a king! She might talk of the lonely days and nights when it looked to everyone else as if she had everything, but inside she felt empty and insignificant. Then came that crossroads moment that changed everything.

I imagine if she had grandchildren they would ask, "Were you afraid?"

"Yes, I was afraid," she would reply.

"Tell us again what you did, Grandma!"

"Well," she would say, "I took my little life to the only person who changes little lives into big ones. I took it to Jehovah God."

So, too, for us, girls.

1. It's time to prepare.

2. We will tuck God's Word deep into our hearts.

3. We will teach our children well.

4. We will fast and pray, for only God knows whether we have come to the kingdom for such a time as this.

CHAPTER NINE

Standing on the Rock

From Despair to Faith

"Axel," replied the Professor with perfect coolness, "our situation is almost desperate; but there are some chances of deliverance, and it is these that I am considering. If at every instant we may perish, so at every instant we may be saved. Let us then be prepared to seize upon the smallest advantage."

—Jules Verne, *Journey to the Center of the Earth*

We now have this light shining in our hearts, but we ourselves are like fragile clay jars containing this great treasure. This makes it clear that our great power is from God, not from ourselves. We are pressed on every side by troubles, but we are not crushed. We are perplexed, but not driven to despair. We are hunted down, but never abandoned by God. We get knocked down, but we are not destroyed. Through suffering, our bodies continue to share in the death of Jesus so that the life of Jesus may also be seen in our bodies.

—2 Corinthians 4:7–10

I n 2007 the *Garfield* cartoon held the record for the world's most widely syndicated comic strip.

Jon Arbuckle is Garfield's fictional owner, a young man with a life fraught with challenges. He dresses too loudly and attempts to alleviate boredom by engaging in such stimulating hobbies as clipping his toenails or buying new socks. He is the butt of most of Garfield's jokes and the recipient of the cat's razor-sharp wit. Preparing for a date one evening, Jon asks Garfield if he thinks his tie is too big, to which the cat replies, "Not at all, as long as your circus friends don't object."[1]

Ouch!

A few years ago Dan Walsh (no relation of mine) introduced a new comic strip, *Garfield Minus Garfield,* in order to reveal Jon's existential inner angst. You might think the cartoon would feel less painful without the barbs of the big orange cat, but you'd be wrong. Somehow, with Garfield in the picture, Jon's despair at least gets heard. In this new strip, however, you feel the loneliness of this young man speaking from a void into a void. (I guess the days of "the funny papers" have passed.)

Even Charles Schulz's beloved *Peanuts* has been given a new twist. Now we have a new strip called *3eanuts* that drops the fourth panel of the traditional four-panel cartoon. The creators explained:

> Charles Schulz's *Peanuts* comics often conceal the existential despair of their world with a closing joke at the characters' expense. With the last panel omitted, despair pervades all.[2]

For example, in one *3eanuts* strip, Charlie Brown approaches Lucy's psychiatric help booth and asks if she can cure loneliness. In panel two, Lucy declares she can cure anything for a nickel. Panel three closes with Charlie Brown asking if she can cure "deep-down, black-bottom-of-the-well, no-hope, end-of-the-world, what's-the-use loneliness." With that, it closes. No funny jab from Lucy, no relief at all.

Despair seems to appeal to those whose taste in comedy runs to the acerbic. I recently discovered a website committed to supporting despair in all its malformations. The creators wrote, "No industry has inflicted more suffering than the Motivational Industry. Motivational books, speakers and posters have made billions of dollars selling shortcuts to success and tools for unleashing our unlimited potential. At Despair, we know such products only raise hopes to dash them. That's why our products go straight to the dashing! Enjoy!"[3]

As the ultimate comedic pessimist, Woody Allen said, "It's not the despair that gets you, it's the hope!" A funny line, maybe, but for many, it hits far from the truth. Despair *does* get them. In fact, despair is all that remains when hope has left the building.

To put it starkly, we need hope to live.

Victor Frankl, describing his observations while caged in a Nazi death camp, wrote, "The prisoner who had lost his faith in the future—his future—was doomed."[4] The Nazis found it far easier to destroy the will to live of someone who no longer saw any reason or purpose for remaining on this earth.

I've heard similar stories from a friend who works with cancer patients. She told me that she has seen patients with very similar diagnoses respond quite differently to treatment, depending on whether they believed they had a good possibility of recovery. With hope, some fight remains in us. Without it, the white flag goes up.

I see despair escalating in our times.

TIMES OF DESPAIR

Recently, on a spring morning in London, I stopped at a pedestrian crossing, waiting for the light to change. I love the sight of the big, red London buses lumbering past. When I lived in London as a student, the outside of the buses usually advertised the latest movie or West End show; but I had never seen anything like I saw that morning. The entire side of the bus featured a large black-and-white poster declaring, "GOD IS DEAD."

It so startled me so much that I missed my light.

Later that day I asked some friends if they had seen these signs. They told me the signs had sprouted up all over London, an advertising campaign sponsored by atheists. What a tragically sad pronouncement over a city!

The English atheists hadn't come up with the slogan, of course. Friedrich Nietzsche—German philosopher, poet, and son of a Lutheran pastor—coined the phrase back in the nineteenth century. What a shock it must have given his father and grandfathers (all three of them pastors) to see this brilliant man not only turn from how he had been raised but basically mock their lives' work! Nietzsche didn't really mean that something terrible had happened to God, but rather that we no longer needed Him. As a culture, we had killed off our weakness or longing to have such a mythic figure to lean on.

Such a belief seemed to offer little comfort to Nietzsche's soul, however. As a young man of forty-five, he had a complete mental breakdown and spent the last eleven years of his life in inner darkness, first in a Basel asylum, then under his mother's care until his death. How that must have tormented his mother, a committed follower of Christ, to watch her son die in such an internal wasteland!

"I Have Tried to Believe"

One of the surest ways for mothers to feel tempted to fall into despair and hopelessness is to have children wander away from or even openly reject faith in Christ. At a recent event, someone pushed an envelope into the side pocket of my briefcase. A mother had scribbled a note on the flip side of a short, typewritten letter, blacking out the signature at the bottom. She wrote only this:

> My son left this note before he killed himself:
> I have tried to believe
> I have tried to hope
> I can't do it anymore
> Please forgive me!

I wept when I read that note. I wept for the boy caught up in such despair that he saw no way out of his pain other than to end his own life. I wept for the mother who could no longer hold her son and tell him that it would be okay. I don't know what was taking place in the life of that young man, but if he were struggling with mental illness, then I know many moments would have come when he could not have lifted his head above the fog.

Those who have never walked such a miserable, dark path cannot possibly understand. Mental illness doesn't show up on an X-ray. The internal mental storms of those who struggle with bipolar disease or schizophrenia resemble nothing else. They change the landscape of the sufferers and make it impossible for them to distinguish between the real and the unreal.

During my own hospitalization with clinical depression, I became very close to a girl who struggled with schizophrenia. As a Christian she loved and trusted God. Even so, this disease had tormented her for years, as it had her mother. The hardest challenge of her life came from how other believers treated her.

Ignorance can supply a cruel, bully pulpit.

She told our group how many people had tried to cast demons out of her. They refused to recognize schizophrenia as a "legitimate disease." Even so, this young woman maintained a pure and simple faith. She told me, "I know that God could heal me in a moment, but I also know that He can hold me when I need to know that He is there and the enemy tells me that I am all alone."

For this darling girl, one word had become her prayer: "Jesus!" When the storm inside raged and she could barely hold on, she had learned to flee to the power found in the name of our risen Savior, Jesus Christ.

MANY PATHS TO DESPAIR

Physical or mental weakness can lead to despair, but many paths can take us there.

"My daughter is back in rehab for the third time—I despair of her
    ever getting clean."
"We have been trying to conceive a child for two years. I despair of
    ever being able to be a mother."
"My husband has been out of work for eighteen months. How will he
    find a new job at his age?"
"My daughter's cancer is back. She's only five years old! Why would
    God let this happen?"

American author Edgar Alan Poe lived a tragic life. He never really knew
his parents. His dad left shortly after his birth, and his mother died before
he turned four. He married his wife, Virginia, when she was just thirteen
(some sources say fourteen), but her death at age twenty-five brought the
final assault. The despair that dogged him shows up clearly in his writings,
but never more so than in his darkest, most famous poem, "The Raven."
It tells the story of a man driven to madness by the death of Lenore, the
woman he loved.

Alone in his room, he hears a tapping at the window. When he throws
open the shutters, the raven flies in. This ominous bird perches on the door
of his chamber and utters one word, "Nevermore." No matter how he questions and questions the bird, the answer remains the same: "Nevermore."
The haunting message of the bird clearly echoes in Poe's broken heart—he
will never see his young wife again. The poem ends this way:

> And my soul from out that shadow that lies floating on the floor
> Shall be lifted—nevermore.

If we have hope only for this life, then we have good reason to despair.
For Christians, however, the glorious truth lies elsewhere. Yes, this life is a
precious gift—but it is fleeting. Our real life remains safe, kept with God,
where no sickness or despair can touch it. Hear the difference in a man who
also faced the loss of those he loved . . . but with faith:

When peace, like a river, attendeth my way,
When sorrows like sea billows roll;
Whatever my lot,
Thou has taught me to say,
It is well; it is well, with my soul.
Though Satan should buffet,
Though trials should come,
Let this blest assurance control,
That Christ has regarded my helpless estate,
And hath shed His own blood for my soul.
And Lord, haste the day when my faith shall be sight,
The clouds be rolled back as a scroll;
The trump shall resound, and the Lord shall descend,
Even so, it is well with my soul.
It is well, with my soul,
It is well, with my soul,
It is well; it is well, with my soul.

This beloved hymn, written by Horatio Spafford after the drowning at sea of his daughters, reflects the hope that refuses to let despair nest.

Yes, despair may barge into your life for a visit, or even a brief stay. But it will not *define* a life that hopes in God.

THE MANY FACES OF DESPAIR

It might help to unpack the ways despair comes at us. Noah Webster defined despair in three ways.

1. Hopelessness—a destitution of hope or expectation
2. That which causes despair; that of which there is no hope
3. Losing hope in the mercy of God.[5]

That third definition takes hopelessness to an achingly dark place that chills me to my core. What a desolate, frightening spot! It sounds like camping on the dark side of the moon. I have known heartache, disappointment, loss, and despair—but not of *that* kind. At times I've lost hope in the mercy of others or the will to extend mercy to myself; but I have never lost hope in God's mercy. I can't even imagine it. That would be a night devoid of light—no moon, no stars, not even any distant, tiny torches flickering in the distance . . . a night utterly dark and tragically quiet.

Webster's third definition gives us a clear distinction that I think we need to bear in mind. He speaks not of losing hope in the existence of God, but of losing hope in His mercy.

I have an anonymous letter on my desk that has prompted me to shed many tears. I have no way of contacting this writer in person, and that makes the pain far worse. I can do nothing but lift her to our Father as she wavers at the cliff's edge of despair:

> The guilt of my four and a half month old son dying of SIDS is killing me.
> I have failed in my marriage and am going through a divorce right now. I
> have a plan of ending my life soon.

This dear sister is drowning in the worst kind of storm, battered by wave after wave of accusation. I can imagine the satanic lies now pounding her:

> *You killed your own child. What kind of mother are you?*
> *Why do you think your husband left? He blames you—they all do!*
> *It would be better if you were dead!*

As I pray for her each day, I call out to God for mercy—what the despairing heart longs for and most needs. If you have tasted that kind of agony, I would love to stop right here and remind you of a few unshakable things.

> The steadfast love of the LORD never ceases;
> his mercies never come to an end;

they are new every morning;

great is your faithfulness. (Lamentations 3:22–23 ESV)

When the enemy tells you that you've gone too far, that you might as well end it all, that no one will care anyway—you need to run to this place of truth and take your stand on it. God's steadfast love *never* ceases. His mercies *never* end. Copy it on a card and carry it with you. Read it over and over again until it begins to become part of the internal fabric of your heart. It may not always *feel* true, but it always *remains* true. Living by faith means pulling what we feel in line with what God has said. As women, our feelings can take us on a roller-coaster ride, but God's Word is the belt of truth that holds us in place.

> But God is so rich in mercy, and he loved us so much, that even though we were dead because of our sins, he gave us life when he raised Christ from the dead. . . .
>
> God saved you by his grace when you believed. And you can't take credit for this; it is a gift from God. Salvation is not a reward for the good things we have done, so none of us can boast about it. For we are God's masterpiece. He has created us anew in Christ Jesus, so we can do the good things he planned for us long ago. (Ephesians 2:4–5, 8–10)

What a description—God's masterpiece! I often feel more like a Picasso painting than a Rembrandt, with a third ear sticking out of my neck and my legs jammed on backward. But Paul remained firm: *God's love is a gift*. We did nothing to earn it and—right in the very teeth of our enemy's lies—we can do nothing to lose it.

SKIRMISHES CONTINUE

But you and I both know that hard questions remain—very real questions that won't go away.

Why can't I have a child?
Why didn't You heal my husband?
Why didn't You stop that drunk driver before he hit and killed my son?

Putting the enemy and his lies in their place and standing on the truth of God's promises—both actions essential—do not fill in all the gaps of the puzzle, do they? A couple of pieces remain missing, but hunt as we will, we just can't find them.

God allows terrible things to happen.
He could stop them and He doesn't.

In light of these two painful realities (which I doubt many who love God would deny), how do we move from despair to faith?

Perhaps before we can start that move, we need to acknowledge yet again that we are at war. In our affluent, relatively secure culture, we can easily get lulled to sleep and forget that a great battle rages all around us—night and day, never ceasing.

As a child, I loved to hear my mother tell stories of living through World War II. She still has her ration book. Food was scarce over the six long years the British nation fought against Adolf Hitler's Germany, and so precious items such as sugar, butter, flour, eggs, and fruit got rationed out according to the numbers of individuals in each family. Every evening, as the sun began to set, my mom and her brothers and sister put up blackout curtains so that German bombers couldn't see even a glimmer of light from a house. She made her way home from Sunday evening services without the benefit of streetlights, and if the air-raid sirens went off, she knew she only had a matter of minutes to get into a shelter before the bombs started falling.

Just a few miles away from her home, a camp held German prisoners of war, captured either from a downed plane or a parachute that landed too close to the home guard. A young German airman once landed right in Mom's backyard and she watched as soldiers arrested him and took him away.

"We never forgot for one moment that we were at war," she would say.

If only I could say the same thing! In my mind—intellectually—I know that we are at war spiritually, but I also want to catch the latest movie or get my nails done. I worry over things like Christian having too much homework or the dog developing a cyst on her paw. We all have such worries; that's life, and we have to live it.

But we must keep one thing always in focus. The cross tells us that although the war is fundamentally over, deadly skirmishes will continue until Christ returns or we go to be with Him. The British novelist H. G. Wells coined the term "The war to end all wars," and US president Woodrow Wilson made it famous as his description of World War I. But the idealistic phrase soon became a thing of derision, for a little more than twenty years after the armistice, an even bigger war broke out.

For us, the cross stands as the war to end all wars, just as the shed blood of Christ became the sacrifice to end all sacrifices. Everything we believe as Christians centers around the cross—but sometimes we forget what the cross accomplished, and so we still live as those who have no hope.

LIVING BY FAITH IN GOD'S MERCY

In his book *Power and Passion*, Simon Wells wrote,

> Sometimes I think if we asked our heavenly Father what the worst part of the cross was, he would pause for a long time and say, "the sacrifice of my only Son . . . that was half of it." And if we waited in terrible silence and finally found courage to ask, "What was the other half?" he would say, "The other half is that 2,000 years later, nobody understands."[6]

I'm not sure God would *really* say such a thing, but I take Wells's point. The cross fully answered the kind of despair that Webster described—losing hope in the mercy of God—but we have to *receive* that hope *by faith*. If only FedEx could deliver hope, how much easier we would find it all!

What does it even look like to be called a woman of faith? If you'd asked me that question as a woman in my twenties or thirties, I think I would have replied, "Someone who never doubts God."

I don't believe that anymore.

I don't think Scripture teaches such an idea either.

Listen to what Hebrews says about a woman who lived way back in the time of Genesis:

> It was by faith that even Sarah was able to have a child, though she was barren and was too old. She believed that God would keep his promise. And so a whole nation came from this one man who was as good as dead—a nation with so many people that, like the stars in the sky and the sand on the seashore, there is no way to count them. (Hebrews 11:11–12)

As I read through this passage again this morning, I found myself talking out loud to the writer. Scholars still debate who wrote the book of Hebrews—Paul? Barnabas? Luke? Apollos?—but my question for the author remains the same: "How long has it been since you read Genesis, buddy?"

Even a quick glance through Genesis reveals a lot more to Sarah's story than "she had faith and believed God." I think it's wonderful that the writer remembered her that way, but we need to take another look at a crucial part of her story. Trust me, she didn't get into Hebrews 11 overnight! If becoming a woman of faith meant that we never wavered or doubted, then Sarah never would have made it into the qualifying rounds. We meet her first in Genesis 11.

> This is the account of Terah's family. Terah was the father of Abram, Nahor, and Haran; and Haran was the father of Lot. But Haran died in Ur of the Chaldeans, the land of his birth, while his father, Terah, was still living. Meanwhile, Abram and Nahor both married. The name of Abram's wife was Sarai, and the name of Nahor's wife was Milcah. (Milcah and her sister Iscah were daughters of Nahor's brother Haran.) (vv. 27–29)

This is more than a sleep-inducing genealogy. Note that when the text lists Terah's children, it gives us the names of just three boys: Abram, Nahor, and Haran. Did you know that he also had a daughter named Sarai? (At this point in the story, their names have not yet changed to Abraham and Sarah.) Although Abram and Sarai had different mothers, Terah fathered them both. In those days the culture didn't value daughters as much as sons, so Sarai got listed simply as Abram's wife.

As if that weren't insult enough, notice the double whammy: "But Sarai was unable to become pregnant and had no children" (11:30). So who was Sarai? How did her people identify her? "She's Abram's wife and she can't have children."

Infertility in the ancient world was a disaster for a woman. Sarai knew the taste of despair! She knew even the kind that Noah Webster described, the loss of hope in the mercy of God. Her culture saw children as a sign of divine blessing, so to have none meant God must have cursed you.

On a first read-through of Sarai's story, we could easily conclude that God looked on her much as the male-dominated culture did. Even the first call that came to Abram said nothing about Sarai:

> The LORD had said to Abram, "Leave your native country, your relatives, and your father's family, and go to the land that I will show you. I will make you into a great nation. I will bless you and make you famous, and you will be a blessing to others. I will bless those who bless you and curse those who treat you with contempt. All the families on earth will be blessed through you." (Genesis 12:1–3)

Notice how many times God uses the word *you*. Not "you and Sarai"; just "you." If you're thinking, *That's not a big deal. Obviously, God meant them both; after all, she was his wife!* True; but did you remember that at this point in the story Abram is seventy-five years old and she is sixty-five? How would any sixty-five-year-old woman who had never been able to conceive think that *she* could possibly be included in such a promise? And if this promise (which clearly seemed to exclude her) seemed enough to engulf Sarai in despair, it would get worse.

As the years passed, Abraham wondered what would happen to everything he possessed if he had no heir. But God made it clear that he would have his very own son.

> Then the LORD said to him, "No, your servant will not be your heir, for you will have a son of your own who will be your heir." (Genesis 15:4)

Sarah already had allowed a lot of things to happen that never should have occurred. She let Abraham hand her over to the king of Egypt, passing her off as his sister (a half-truth). Not quite "woman of faith" material yet! And when she heard from Abraham that God had promised him an heir, Sarah became desperate.

Despair can make us do crazy things. Have you ever been there? You know that God has promised to provide what you need, but His timing differs radically from yours, so you take things into your own hands. A friend of mine got so tired of waiting for a Christian husband that she went ahead and married a guy with no faith at all. I could see despair etched into the little lines around her eyes. Despair makes us rationalize:

If I don't get married now, I'll never be able to have children.
If I don't give this guy what he wants, I'll lose him.
If I don't take action, I'll never get such a chance again.

My friend signed up for a lot of heartache for a lot of years. So did Sarah.

The culture of Sarah's day accepted surrogate motherhood, and so Sarah urged Abraham to sleep with her servant, Hagar. He did, and nine months later Hagar gave birth to a boy, Ishmael. You can read the whole story in Genesis 15, but you can summarize the decision in one word.

Disaster!

While everyone sees the boy as Abraham's son, nobody recognizes him as belonging to Sarah. Ishmael comes into her home in her seventy-sixth year—and thirteen years of silence follow.

Silence. Is anything harder to bear? For thirteen long, torturous years, Sarah has to watch Abraham play with a boy that is not hers.

God has forgotten me.

On your knees, you have placed your urgent requests before God. And what do you get? Silence.

You pray for a husband. Silence.

You beg for a child. Silence.

You need a job. Silence.

You ask God for a sign that He is with you. Silence.

Silence feels like solitary confinement. You knock at a door that never opens. You call a number that rings and rings and rings and never gets answered, not even by a machine. You scream into a canyon without getting back so much as an echo. You sit alone, in the dark, and not even crickets keep you company. Sarah could do nothing as the silent years marched by.

Do you see why I questioned the writer to the Hebrews? Not much in the story to this point qualifies Sarah for the Hall of Faith . . . and there's something great about that.

We see our failures and our lack of faith, but *God* sees what we will become as His Spirit faithfully works through the broken pieces of our lives. God's timing always perfectly matches His plans, even if sometimes it runs roughshod over ours—something Sarah was about to see.

> Then God said to Abraham, "Regarding Sarai, your wife—her name will no longer be Sarai. From now on her name will be Sarah. And I will bless her and give you a son from her!" (Genesis 17:15–16)

Finally, God spoke her name!

Her file had *not* gotten lost in some back office of heaven. Sarah, at eighty-nine years of age, at last learned of the plan that God had put in place long before. She became pregnant with a son, Isaac, and gave birth at age ninety. Imagine if such a thing happened today. She'd be on the *Dr. Phil* show!

Sarah was a woman of faith, someone who endured the storms of life that are not unlike those that hit each one of us. A woman of faith holds fast to the truth, even when nothing seems to make sense to her, knowing that her faith stands (and rests) on the finished work of Christ.

So what can the mother do whose son held on to hope for as long as he could before taking his own life? What answer can she give when the enemy lies, *It's all over?* I recommend a very short one: *"No!"*

Because of Christ, we may lose a battle, but we still win the war.

STANDING THROUGH YOUR STORM

So what can you and I take away from Sarah's story?

1. Sarah teaches us to not let despair make our decisions. When you feel that urgent, churning-in-your-soul panic, insisting that you just *have* to do something now or burst—stop. Wait on God. Ask Him to restore hope in the midst of the storm.

Do you remember how the psalmist David used to speak to himself when he felt the cold fingers of despair?

> Why am I discouraged?
>> Why is my heart so sad?
> I will put my hope in God!
>> I will praise him again—
>> my Savior and my God!
>
> Now I am deeply discouraged,
>> but I will remember you. (Psalm 42:5–6)

2. When you feel that you can't hold on for one more moment, then remember Paul's words: "The temptations in your life are

no different from what others experience. And God is faithful. He will not allow the temptation to be more than you can stand. When you are tempted, he will show you a way out so that you can endure" (1 Corinthians 10:13).

3. Just as God always had Sarah in His loving, merciful hands, so He has a good, strong hold on you. When you feel overwhelmed by despair, Peter reminds you where to take it: "Give all your worries and cares to God, for he cares about you" (1 Peter 5:7).

4. The most potent way to put despair firmly in its place is to build a gut-firm conviction of the reality of heaven, and *not* simply a passing acknowledgment of a better place somewhere, someday. That's what Paul meant when he wrote,

We are pressed on every side by troubles, but we are not crushed. We are perplexed, but not driven to despair. We are hunted down, but never abandoned by God. We get knocked down, but we are not destroyed. Through suffering, our bodies continue to share in the death of Jesus so that the life of Jesus may also be seen in our bodies. (2 Corinthians 4:8–10)

That is our eternal hope! And God's mercy is our eternal companion.

Father God,

I believe that on the cross despair was dealt a lethal blow. But sometimes it still washes over me and I feel my hope drowning. Help me remember what *is* true no matter what *feels* true for a moment. Thank You that my hope is in You and You will never leave me.

Amen.

CHAPTER TEN

On a Clear Day We Can See Home

From Rage to Restoration

I was angry with my friend:
I told my wrath, my wrath did end.
I was angry with my foe:
I told it not, my wrath did grow.

—William Blake, *Songs of Experience*

Therefore, having put away falsehood, let each one of you speak the truth with his neighbor, for we are members one of another. Be angry and do not sin; do not let the sun go down on your anger, and give no opportunity to the devil.

—Ephesians 4:25–27 (ESV)

At five years of age, our son, Christian, developed a coping mechanism that both alarmed and entertained us.

If he felt frustrated, he would hold his breath, blow out his little cheeks, and clench his fists until he got so flushed he looked ready to pop. I tried to get him to stop, but he became so attached to this new

179

behavior he would watch himself in the mirror, like an actor studying for opening night.

"Baby, why do you do that holding-your-breath thing?" I asked him one morning at breakfast.

He looked up at me with his big, brown, emotive eyes and said, "Mommy, don't you ever feel that if something doesn't change, you might just burst?"

I still do. I think at times, we all do. From the mouths of babes, right? I totally understood where he was coming from, even at age five.

One of the most challenging things about living on a broken planet is that so many things make us feel we might just burst if they don't change. Whether you feel as though your child has received unfair treatment at school, your husband is being passed over for promotion in his job, or "that woman" keeps getting asked to do things at church when so many others seem just as willing and capable—life has more than its share of self-combustible moments.

I once received an irate call from a mom whose daughter went to school with Christian. She could hardly talk to me through her rage and tears. She sputtered that Christian had thrown a ball to his friend, but he had missed his target and knocked her daughter off a swing. The girl was fine, but the mom seemed beside herself. I listened until she had spent her fury, and then told her I'd look into it. When I asked if I could pray for her, she began to sob.

Sometimes it takes only one final, little thing to push us right off the edge. If we are "stuffers"—and many of us are—we push down major assault after major assault, and the stack of wood grows higher and higher until one little spark hits and BAM!

Tears of pure frustration often accompany those moments, because we know something more is going on inside than just the fact that for the third time this week the dryer has mysteriously taken several socks to the missing sock planet. Frustration not dealt with can become anger, which, when ignored, can suddenly and unexpectedly ramp up to rage.

How many of the arguments you have with your husband and kids feel a bit out of control, out of proportion? Yes, it annoys you when your teenage son keeps fossilized sandwiches in his room and your husband can never seem to move his underwear that final twenty feet from the floor into the laundry basket, but the way we feel about these situations often indicates that much more boils and bubbles just beneath the surface.

And very rarely is it "underwear anger."

Frustration can open the door to anger and rage. When we feel powerless, we find it all too easy to stuff our emotions deep into the cellars of our souls. But when we do that, we just add to what my friend (and dramatist) Nicole Johnson calls "fuel dumps." We unwittingly saturate our souls with accelerant. May God have mercy on the one who innocently flips a match on top of the pile!

A Road to Darker Places

A strong sense of frustration and rage can lead to far darker places than losing it on the phone. Recent studies into school bullying and violence tell stories of young men and girls who feel they have no voice.

> Most students involved in violent acts in schools, from Columbine to the most recent act in Elmira, N.Y., where a student brought bombs and guns to school, were alienated and did not have a sense of belonging with the school or other students. Alienation, isolation, verbal abuse, all [work] to provide rage in a person and [contribute] to latent hostility—a sense of getting even when no one is looking.[1]

Since the massacre in Newtown, Connecticut, public outrage has reached an all-time high. When something makes no sense to us, we have an innate need to point a finger, to find a reason for why the unreasonable happened. If we have someone to blame, we feel a bit more in control; if we can punish him, perhaps the bad things won't happen again. In the days and weeks that followed the Sandy Hook Elementary School shooting, outraged citizens mounted platforms of various kinds to deliver passionate and convincing speeches.

"We need proper gun control!"

"Guns don't kill people . . . people kill people."

"You took God out of our schools, and this is what happens!"

No matter the rights or wrongs of these arguments, I found it hard to listen to impassioned speeches while families buried their children.

It is easy and tempting to simply politicize the rage that leads to such tragedies, but it's not a party issue—it is a disease of the human heart.

What Does God Say About Anger?

I've said we find our hope at the throne of mercy—but do we, as Christian women, take our anger there?

Anger tends to make us feel uncomfortable. While our society often perceives an angry man as passionate and strong, more often than not it perceives an angry woman as out of control (and often calls her a word that rhymes with "witch").

God's Word has a lot to say about anger. It portrays anger as both justifiable and unjustifiable.

We get a picture of righteous anger when Moses came down from Mount Sinai after receiving the Ten Commandments. His anger burned when he saw a scene of blatant idol worship among His people.

> And as soon as he came near the camp and saw the calf and the dancing, Moses' anger burned hot, and he threw the tablets out of his hands and broke them at the foot of the mountain. He took the calf that they had made and burned it with fire and ground it to powder and scattered it on the water and made the people of Israel drink it. (Exodus 32:19–20 esv)

In the early life of King Saul, we see that the Holy Spirit can prompt anger:

And the Spirit of God rushed upon Saul when he heard these words, and his anger was greatly kindled. (1 Samuel 11:6 ESV)

In the life of Christ, we see righteous anger perfectly portrayed:

And he said to the man with the withered hand, "Come here." And he said to them, "Is it lawful on the Sabbath to do good or to do harm, to save life or to kill?" But they were silent. And he looked around at them with anger, grieved at their hardness of heart, and said to the man, "Stretch out your hand." He stretched it out, and his hand was restored. (Mark 3:3–5 ESV)

Christ felt angry that the letter of the law had taken the place of mercy. And it angered Him that those whom God had ordained to serve as channels of divine mercy had totally missed the point.

Scripture also gives us a template for recognizing out-of-control and ungodly anger:

The LORD accepted Abel and his gift, but he did not accept Cain and his gift. This made Cain very angry, and he looked dejected.

"Why are you so angry?" the LORD asked Cain. "Why do you look so dejected? You will be accepted if you do what is right. But if you refuse to do what is right, then watch out! Sin is crouching at the door, eager to control you. But you must subdue it and be its master." (Genesis 4:4–7)

Commentators have suggested a variety of reasons to explain why God did not accept Cain's offering. Some say he failed to offer a blood sacrifice; but even the Mosaic code, introduced long afterward, stipulated many sacrifices that did not involve blood. My own theory is that his heart had gone awry. God saw the ungodly competition that stirred in Cain's heart, and also where it could lead. So God warned Cain and gave him a chance to shift, but he refused; and so instead of mastering his anger, it mastered him, leading him to murder his brother.

Scripture clearly links the ability to master anger with submission to the Holy Spirit. The more we harden our hearts against the voice that calls us back to the Father's heart on bended knee, the farther from grace and salvation we wander.

We see this principle profoundly illustrated in the life of King Saul, one of the greatest tragedies of the Old Testament.

THE JEALOUSY-ANGER CONNECTION

Saul, the first king of Israel, had a lot going for him, but the enemy knew Saul's weaknesses and played on them fiercely. The vain Saul had a mean jealous streak—and jealousy, given free rein, leads to disaster.

A shepherd boy named David once stood before Saul and told him that although fear kept every man in the king's army from fighting Goliath, he would battle the giant. He faced this freakish, monster-soldier alone and brought him down with one stone, placed strategically between the eyes. David grew to love Saul, and when he saw the king wrestling with his internal demons, he would play on his harp, providing Spirit-inspired worship to soothe the king and restore hope.

Saul would have, could have, should have become a magnificent king.

But if God had a plan for his life, so did the enemy. And the two agendas were as different as could be. Satan intended to destroy this king and at the same time bring down David, God's chosen one. I can only imagine the festering filth he stirred up within King Saul.

See that boy? He intends to take your place.
Look at how your people love him!
He's getting more popular every day—you'll
have to do something about that.

Let me say it again: jealousy, given free rein, always leads to disaster. The Bible records how Saul allowed his mind to grow so polluted by satanic lies that he could no longer discern the truth.

Saul boiled with rage at Jonathan. "You stupid son of a whore!" he swore at him. "Do you think I don't know that you want him to be king in your place, shaming yourself and your mother? As long as that son of Jesse is alive, you'll never be king. Now go and get him so I can kill him!"

"But why should he be put to death?" Jonathan asked his father. "What has he done?" Then Saul hurled his spear at Jonathan, intending to kill him. So at last Jonathan realized that his father was really determined to kill David. (1 Samuel 20:30–33)

Out-of-control anger, spurred on by the enemy of God, will always bring us down. Consider one of the saddest verses in the entire canon of Scripture: "Now the Spirit of the LORD had left Saul" (1 Samuel 16:14). Saul refused to bend the knee to God, and the Lord left him to stew in his own bile.

When we resist the Spirit and submit to our own broken humanity, we lose, every time. Saul forgot that he served a sovereign God. He forgot that as long as God had not finished with him, it wouldn't matter how many armies marched against him; he would prevail.

We take our eyes off our Father at our own peril. When we harden our hearts, as Saul did, and refuse God's mercy and grace, we lose something else in the bargain: His goodness and His truth.

Saul had no reason left to live. Fear of man had replaced fear of God—a dismal exchange. While fear of God brings us to a safe and strong place, fear of man leads inevitably to desolation and terror.

Saul groaned to his armor bearer, "Take your sword and kill me before these pagan Philistines come to run me through and taunt and torture me." But his armor bearer was afraid and would not do it. So Saul took his own sword and fell on it. (1 Samuel 31:4)

When jealousy or rage besiege us—and chances are, they will at some point in our lives—we need to remember where they come from and run to God for help. As women we have to consciously, by God's grace, fight this beast. Jealousy is a fierce foe that often presents itself as a supporter. The enemy's lies are not always easy to recognize.

> *Why does she get all the attention when God*
> *has given you so much to say?*
> *You should speak up and put her in her place . . .*
> *for the good of the whole church.*

Giving in to those lies that lead to division and destruction produces a spiritual death inside of us. Like Saul, we get to choose: will we fall on our own sword or fall on the mercy of God? Bringing this aspect of our humanity under the sovereignty of God could mean the difference between spiritual life or death for every one of us. Jealousy is a finely tuned barb straight from the pit of hell, and we allow it to rest inside us at our peril.

WHAT TO DO WITH ANGER

As I write, I'm looking at several e-mails, each one related to anger. Listen to the pain and strain in this one:

> I divorced my husband because of the affair he had. I was so angry. Then after his affair, I had one, too, because I felt I deserved to ruin someone else's life. I just ruined my own.

I wish that were the only such note, but I have many more:

> "I am so angry and bitter. I can't and won't forgive."
> "I can't believe my husband cheated on me with her. I was so angry I put my fist through the wall in our bedroom and ended up in the emergency room."
> "I have so much hatred toward others. My life is a mess, so I turn to drugs to help. I am lost."

"I am so full of rage for the disability I was born with. So much pain, unforgiveness, shame . . . my inability to live with my disability."

"I am so angry with my father for leaving when I was young. I will never forgive him."

What do we do with these "fuel dumps"? Scripture tells us three crucial things:

1. Be slow to anger (James 1:19).
2. Be angry but don't sin (Ephesians 4:26).
3. Put away anger (Ephesians 4:31).

But *how*? How do we do it? How do we obey? When anger boils deep inside, rumbling and threatening to erupt like a sleeping volcano, how do we pull ourselves back from the brink? How can we line ourselves up with God's Word again? How do we even discover where that lava-like rage comes from?

Let me tell you a story about a woman who is very dear to me. I tell her story with her permission. Her name is Davina.

ACT I

Davina wasn't thrilled about her name. It had belonged to her paternal grandmother, and by all accounts, the woman was a piece of work.

"Why would you call me after a woman who was so mean and spiteful?" she asked her mother one day.

"Well, your sister was called after my mother, so it seemed only right," her mother replied.

Thank goodness my grandfather wasn't Adolf Hitler, or goodness knows what my brother would be saddled with! she thought.

Davina *thought* a lot of things; she just never said them out loud. She had lost that right a long time before when she had ruined the lives of everyone in her family. She didn't mean to—children seldom do—but it happened anyway.

Whenever her daddy got mean, she became more vigilant. She considered it her job to contain and absorb his anger, because she knew and loved him like no one else. But one day her system failed her. A five-year-old child can handle only so much. He meant to extinguish her that day in his rage, but she fought back—a decision she regretted for most of her life. Authorities removed him from the home and, in despair, he took his own life. No one told Davina exactly what had happened. She knew only that her mom came home one day in a black dress and a black hat, took all the pictures off the wall and the bureau, and put them in a suitcase under the bed. She knew that her mother never wore black . . . she hated herself in black.

This must be a hate-filled day, Davina thought.

ACT 2

Act 2 began as though Act 1 had never occurred. No one spoke about the incident. Davina imagined that they all talked about it but stopped whenever she came into the room. And it stopped, she knew, because it was her fault.

No one ever said they actually *blamed* her. They just looked sad all the time, which felt much worse. So she worked very hard to make life easier for everyone else. Even when someone asked her to do jobs not her own, she did them. She had to, right? She had lost the right to speak because of what she had done. A lifetime would not compensate for her failure.

On the night Davina gave her life to Christ, she got much more than she bargained for. God gave Davina a second chance. She discovered on that evening that not only did she have a relationship with Jesus, but she had a new Father as well. And she would *not* fail this Father, *no matter what.*

No matter what.

No matter *what*!

ACT 3

If she looked in a mirror, Davina could see why others thought of her as a grown woman. She wore a squeaky-clean disguise, and she knew all her lines.

"Of course I'll do that. No problem."

"They didn't show up? Don't worry . . . I'll do it."

"You're right; I didn't do well today. I'm *so* sorry."

"I totally understand why you find it hard to love me. I do too."

Contained. Davina liked that word. The world felt safer to her when she stayed inside a container. Yes, it also felt a bit cold and lonely; but that seemed only right for someone who'd done what she had done.

Safe

Contained

Keep smiling

Say yes!

ACT 4

Tired. Davina felt *so* very tired. It had become harder and harder to think clearly. She stood at the ATM, staring at the keypad.

What are the four digits? Come on, you know this.

She watched the bank machine consume her card . . . and knew it had just begun. She was a grown woman who couldn't remember four simple digits. She was beginning to crumble from the inside out.

Whispers followed her everywhere she went. Some stares looked sympathetic; others, as if she were unclean. Only one question remained: "What does the circus do when the show is over? It turns off the lights."

ACT 5

"I want you to look at this chart and let me know which emotions you are feeling right now," he said.

Davina tried to focus on the doctor's voice. She looked at the chart. It didn't seem to be in English.

Shame

Fear

Loneliness

Anger

Sadness

"I don't know what you mean," she said finally, too tired to try and get it right.

"When you look at this," he explained, "are you sad . . . afraid? What do you feel right now?"

Davina looked at the chart and then at him. "I don't feel anything."

But he wouldn't let it go.

She should have warned him.

Did no one tell him about her? He just wouldn't stop.

Davina picked up a chair and threw it across the room with enough force to stop an army. "*That's* how I feel," she roared. "Will that do?"

"That's very good," he said with the kindest smile she had ever seen. "Now we can begin."

ACT 6

"My name is Sheila Davina Walsh, and I have no idea why I am here." That was my opening line in my first morning group devotional with ten other patients. Their lines sounded much better.

"I'm John, and I'm here because I tried to take my own life because . . . I think I'm gay and I don't know what to do with that."

"I'm Sarah, and I'm here because I won't eat. I think I'm fat, but I weigh ninety-two pounds."

That was the first morning of my journey back to life, from rage to restoration.

The truth is, I have lived with buried anger and fear since I was five years old. I never looked like I was angry or afraid. I learned to hide it, but it was always just under the surface. My father's illness and subsequent violent behavior had nothing to do with me, but I loved him with all my five-year-old heart, so I didn't "get" that. I knew only that instead of letting him bring his cane down on my head, I pulled it away from him, and he fell on the floor, screaming like an animal. Men in white coats took him away that day, and he died at thirty-four years of age in the river behind the psychiatric hospital where he had gone as a patient.

I *knew* it was my fault. If I had just stood there and taken it, my mom would still have a husband and my brother and sister would still have a dad. But I chose to live . . . and I had to pay for that decision. Growing up, that's what I believed. But a part of me felt ferociously angry that I believed it.

> The weight of this sad time we must obey.
> Speak what we feel, not what we ought to say.
> —WILLIAM SHAKESPEARE, *KING LEAR*

The truth is, bad things happen in this world—and so often we take the weight on ourselves. It almost kills us. It almost took me out.

I felt angry that my dad hurt me.

I felt angry that men took him away and I had to live in a family with such a huge missing piece.

I felt angry that he killed himself and left me with the fallout of his choice.

But most of all, I felt angry with myself, because I abandoned that brave little five-year-old girl who dared to fight back. I punished her for surviving by putting her in the cellar.

Do you know the greatest gift I received during my one-month stay in a psychiatric hospital? I began to understand that it is all right just to be human and to tell the truth before the shame consumed me.

My doctor suggested that I write a letter to my dad. I reminded him that my dad had died quite some time ago, but he persisted.

"Write it all down. Don't edit yourself. Just let it go."

At first, I felt foolish. But as I began to write, it seemed as though I had unstopped a river. Everything began to flow, and I told my dad about it all. When I finished, I had a hard time reading some of it, as my tears had blurred the pages. I had never done anything so brutally honest—and I knew I wanted to go back to where it all began. I had never visited my father's grave. My mom had gone just once: the day she buried him. She never visited again.

I flew home to Scotland to discover that no headstone marked my dad's grave. Mom did not remember where, in this vast cemetery, they had laid his body. I thought I had hit a brick wall until I discovered a plot number in our town's records assigned to my father.

I found the place.

I remember that day as if it were yesterday. I sat beside the small piece of land that served as my dad's final resting place. I read the letter out loud, and by the time I finished, my head was resting on the grass. I could say only, "I'm so sorry, Dad!"

But it was a different kind of "sorry" this time. I didn't feel sorry that I had lived; I felt sorry for his deep brokenness and his illness. And I forgave us both. I left with my father that day, my relationship with him restored more than thirty years after it had shattered when I was five.

For years I was too afraid to allow myself to be angry because of where it might lead. I didn't understand that the greatest danger is when we don't deal with it but stuff it deep down into the basement of our lives. I thought containing it was good, but in essence I ended up containing everything—joy, peace, hope, love, and life.

I left the subject of rage to restoration to the very last chapter for a couple of reasons.

One, it's deeply personal. For years I believed the lie of the enemy that it was that one moment when I allowed myself to fight back and live that destroyed my family. It was as if I chose to put my heart into a coma. A friend of mine was put into a medically induced coma for a few days to let his body recover from traumatic injury. As he began to heal, the doctors brought him out of his coma; but when you do it to yourself, you're stuck. That's what I thought, anyway. I was wrong. There is a Great Physician who is stronger and more compassionate than we will ever understand. He is the One who brings dead things back to life. I am a witness to that truth.

The second reason I left this to the end is that I hoped you might trust me a little by now, for this is a hard subject to deal with, and yet all the time, I meet women just like I was. The rage is contained, but every now and then it leaks out. Of all the emotions that we deal with as women, this has the most potent power and is the most difficult to talk about. When we feel it begin to stir, it's like a vortex, a whirlpool that might drag us under the water and we will not survive. I understand these feelings. I know that there are days when you would like to put your fist through the wall, but you just do one more load of laundry and move on. Rage frightens us.

What if we take it out on our children?
What if we say something, do something, and we can't take it back?
What if we ruin everything?
What if the storm inside us is too great to be contained?

Let's stop here, girls, and declare together that is a lie from the pit of hell. The enemy wants to keep us in an underwater prison of rage, believing that we are lost, hopeless.

We are not lost.
We are not hopeless.
We are redeemed.

Christ paid everything so that we can live; not just survive—live!

At sixteen I was cast in a school play that dealt with the emotions in the soul of a man who was about to commit murder. I was given the role of anger. I found the role claustrophobic, draped from head to toe in red net that tightened around my ankles as I moved. The playwright had written it in such a way that no one else on stage could control me. Fear was too weak, so I sent her packing. Logic was cold and easy to ignore. The final moments of the play were devastating—because I won.

I understand that play all too well. If you struggle with rage, the great fear is that ultimately no one will be able to control you and it will win. To that fear I say this,

You are a defeated foe.
You still feel powerful, but your power is an illusion, because on the cross,
    Christ dealt a deathblow to you.
I am not strong, but I rest in the shadow of the One who took the worst
    you had to throw and rose again victorious.
In Jesus' name—you lose!

> Masterstrokes across a canvas
> Bold moves—color splashes everywhere
> Unfettered and full of dreams
> Beneath His brush the canvas comes to life
> Awesome, intimate
> I stand amazed
> Then He dips my finger in the paint and I become a part
> It's like I'm finger painting with Picasso
> And as God takes my hand the paint on his runs into mine
> A new color is born

(JOURNAL ENTRY)

STANDING THROUGH YOUR STORM

As I bring this book to a close, I am praying for you. I don't know and I can't imagine the pain, the loss, the injury you have absorbed into the fabric of your soul. But may I tell you one of the greatest lessons I have learned in my life? God is big enough to handle *all* our stuff. I learned it in stages.

1. Learn to trust God as the One to whom you can tell everything. In every relationship we choose what we share. But with God, pour it all out. You will never know a friend like Christ!

2. If you feel angry, turn to Him. Don't deny your anger or machine-gun those around you with your pain. Talk it all through with God first. Find a quiet spot, and yell if it helps—just let it all out. Pour out the rage and the brokenness until you feel spent.

3. Then let Him hold and comfort you. The enemy must find it horrid and detestable when we trust God enough to tell Him the whole truth!

Lord Jesus Christ,
    Thank You for loving me, for loving all of me.
    Thank You for inviting me to come and pour my pain at Your feet.
    I bring the rage that has been buried deep inside to You and leave it there.
    I am loved, I am restored, I am redeemed!
    Amen.

EPILOGUE

DAUGHTERS OF THE ONE WHO SPEAKS TO STORMS

A good soldier in an enemy's country should everywhere and at all times be on the alert. It has been one of the rules of my life, and if I have lived to wear grey hairs it is because I have observed it.
—SIR ARTHUR CONAN DOYLE, *THE ADVENTURES OF GERARD*

Let the morning bring me word of your unfailing love,
for I have put my trust in you.
Show me the way I should go,
for to you I entrust my life.

—PSALM 143:8 (NIV)

I have finally come up with a good answer for that annoying question, "Tell us something about yourself that our audience might not know."

My son makes me carry a Swiss Army knife when I take our dogs for a walk at night. It's ridiculous, I know, but it makes him feel better.

It all started with the sighting of a bobcat in our neighbor's backyard. The animal just sat there one morning on top of their grill, as if about to make a speech. My neighbor screamed, the bobcat shrieked, and my dogs went bonkers. The morning became infinitely more interesting than normal as we watched this brown-gray beauty disappear into the woods.

That night, as usual, I called Belle and Tink for their evening promenade. As I put on their leashes, Christian appeared with lethal weapon in hand.

"What's that for?" I asked as he proffered his trusty blade.

"It's for protection, Mom," he said. "That bobcat is out there somewhere, lurking."

"How do you know it's lurking?" I wondered aloud.

"It's what they do, Mom—they lurk!"

I looked at the pocket-sized knife and wondered how I would fare using it against a pouncing, lurking, toothy beast.

"If it sees you have a weapon," he continued, "it's more likely to run off." He spoke with the confident assurance of one about to send his well-equipped mother into battle.

I'm happy to report I've never had to use the knife, so the bobcat's pride remains intact. But every time I see that penknife sitting beside the leashes at the front door, I am reminded that a battle rages around us every moment of every day. We put down our weapons at our own peril.

We are aliens on this earth. This is not our home. And the dark prince who rules here is hell-bent on our destruction—but God has equipped us with mighty weapons of warfare.

In our skirts or skinny jeans, we may not look like mighty warriors to the casual observer, but listen to me, daughters of the King: we are a force to be reckoned with! As Paul wrote to the church in Corinth,

> For though we live in the world, we do not wage war as the world does. The weapons we fight with are not the weapons of the world. On the contrary, they have divine power to demolish strongholds. (2 Corinthians 10:3–4 NIV)

In this book we have unpacked many of the issues that the enemy uses to torment us. If he could, he would use them to cause us to fall away from faith in Christ. But in the name and power of the risen and soon returning Lord Jesus Christ, we will *not* fall away! When we make a commitment to no longer live by what we *feel* is true but by what God's Word tells us is true, we can stand in the strongest storms of life.

I urge you, my dear sister, to build up an armory of the Word of God deep inside your spirit. Tuck prayers into every piece of laundry. Anoint every doorpost in your home, praying that any who enter would feel the peace and presence of Christ.

Scripture makes it clear that no one but the Father knows the hour of Christ's return. But when He comes again, I want to be ready and waiting and fighting and watching for His appearance. Until He comes, storms will continue to howl inside—but we follow the One who speaks to storms and bids them be still. You are not alone! You never have been, and you never will be. God is at work all night long through even the darkest storm.

In 1956 Cecil B. DeMille directed the epic movie *The Ten Commandments,* in which the Hebrew-born Moses, an adopted Egyptian prince, becomes the deliverer of the Hebrew slaves. It's hard to forget that moment when Charlton Heston, cast as Moses, raises his staff over the Red Sea and the waters part in seventeen seconds. It was a moment of pure drama back in 1956, but it's not the way it happened. The way it actually happened is far more meaningful to us as we face life's inevitable storms. We read the story in Exodus 14.

> Then Moses stretched out his hand over the sea, and the Lord drove the sea back by a strong east wind all night and made the sea dry land, and the waters were divided. And the people of Israel went into the midst of the sea on dry ground, the waters being a wall to them on their right hand and on their left. (Exodus 14:21–22 ESV)

All night long! It didn't happen in a moment. God was working all night long through the darkness. We don't know how long the night will be, but we do know this: no matter how things appear, God is at work—all night long! Only the morning light will reveal what God has done. Do not despair or give in to the chaos of what you feel. Stand strong on what you know is true. Our Savior has gone ahead to prepare a place for us, and He will return and take us home. Stand strong and hold your head up high! You are royalty! You are a daughter of the King of all kings!

Let me leave you with the beautiful charge that Paul gave to his dear disciple, Timothy.

I solemnly urge you in the presence of God and Christ Jesus, who will someday judge the living and the dead when he appears to set up his Kingdom: Preach the word of God. Be prepared, whether the time is favorable or not. Patiently correct, rebuke, and encourage your people with good teaching.

For a time is coming when people will no longer listen to sound and wholesome teaching. They will follow their own desires and will look for teachers who will tell them whatever their itching ears want to hear. They will reject the truth and chase after myths.

But you should keep a clear mind in every situation. Don't be afraid of suffering for the Lord. Work at telling others the Good News, and fully carry out the ministry God has given you.

As for me, my life has already been poured out as an offering to God. The time of my death is near. I have fought the good fight, I have finished the race, and I have remained faithful. And now the prize awaits me—the crown of righteousness, which the Lord, the righteous Judge, will give me on the day of his return. And the prize is not just for me but for all who eagerly look forward to his appearing. (2 Timothy 4:1–8)

Acknowledgments

Sheila would like to thank the following people for their invaluable help in writing this book:

Steve Halliday and Larry Libby. I have learned so much from both of you on the fine art of writing. You take my thoughts and ideas and help me present them in such a way that they are accessible to all. Thank you!

Bryan Norman. You have moved on now to new opportunities but I am deeply grateful for the work you did on this book. More than that, you have been a cheerleader, a faithful critic, and a dear friend.

Brian Hampton. My life continues to be graced and stretched by your leadership and support.

Janene MacIvor and the editorial staff at Thomas Nelson, who push for excellence and work so hard to make it happen.

Julie Allen and James Phinney. For the creative and effective cover and interior design.

Chad Cannon, Stephanie Tresner, and Emily Lineberger. It's a joy to work with you. I love your passion and commitment to get the message out to as many people as possible with great clarity.

Esther Fedorkevich and the staff at the Fedd Agency. It's an honor to be represented by you who represent Christ and His kingdom so well.

Women of Faith. This is my eighteenth year serving on stage with some of the most amazing sisters and friends I could ever hope for. We have welcomed in our five millioneth guest and seen more than 366,000 women surrender their lives to Christ. I can't wait to see what God has in store for us this year. Revival!

As always my love and gratitude and heart belong to my husband, Barry, and our darling son, Christian.

The deepest allegiance of my heart and life will always be to my Lord and Savior, Jesus Christ, the one to whom every storm must bow.

"He calmed the storm to a whisper and stilled the waves. What a blessing was that stillness as he brought them safely into harbor!"
Psalms 107:28–29 (NLT)

NOTES

CHAPTER 1: WHEN A TSUNAMI HITS THE HEART: FROM HEARTBREAK TO STRENGTH

1. Gabriel José de la Concordia García Márquez; for biography visit http://www .goodreads.com/author/show/13450.Gabriel_Garc_a_M_rquez.

CHAPTER 2: A LONG, DARK WINTER: FROM DISAPPOINTMENT TO HOPE

1. Herman Melville, Letter to Nathaniel Hawthorne, June 1851, http://xroads.virginia .edu/~ma96/atkins/cmletter.html.
2. Miroslav Volf, *The End of Memory: Remembering Rightly in a Violent World* (Grand Rapids: Wm. B. Eerdmans, 2006).

CHAPTER 3: NAVIGATING TREACHEROUS WATERS: FROM UNFORGIVENESS TO FREEDOM

1. Michael Duduit, *Handbook of Contemporary Preaching* (Nashville: Broadman Press, 1992), 175.
2. Robert J. Morgan, *Nelson's Complete Book of Stories, Illustrations and Quotes* (Nashville: Thomas Nelson, 2000), 312.
3. R. T. Kendall, *Total Forgiveness* (Lake Mary, FL: Charisma House, 2002).
4. Dick Tibbits, *Forgive to Live* (Nashville, TN: Integrity Publishers, 2006), 91.
5. Ibid., 97.

CHAPTER 4: COVERED BY CHRIST: FROM SHAME TO LOVE

1. Quote from www.alienyoutharmy.com/annie-lobert-testimony-video/.
2. To hear Annie Lobert's story, visit, http://www.iamsecond.com/seconds /annie-lobert/.
3. Edward T Welch, *Shame Interrupted* (Greensboro, NC: New Growth Press, 2012).
4. Ibid.
5. For more information on Annie's ministry, visit http://hookersforJesus.net.

Chapter 5: A Silent Storm: From Regret to Rest
1. www.theA21campaign.org.

Chapter 6: Thunder and Lightning: From Fear to Joy
1. Ronald C. Kessler et al.,"Lifetime prevalence and age-of-onset distributions of mental disorders in the World Health Organization's World Mental Health Survey Initiative," *World Psychiatry*, 6, no. 3 (October 2007): 168–176, http://www.ncbi .nlm.nih.gov/pmc/articles/PMC2174588/.

Chapter 7: From Battered to Beautiful: From Insecurity to Confidence
1. http://www.victimsofcrime.org/news-center/reporter-resources/child-sexual-abuse /child-sexual-abuse-statistics.
2. Sheila Walsh, *Honestly* (Grand Rapids: Zondervan, 1997).
3. Nancy Haught, The National Center for Victims of Crime, "Child Sexual Abuse Statistics," *The Oregonian*, February 10, 2013, L1, http://www.oregonlive.com /living/index.ssf/2013/02/just_in_time_for_lent_a_new_se.html.
4. William MacDonald, *Believers Bible Commentary*, ed. Arthur Farsad (Nashville: Thomas Nelson, 1989).

Chapter 8: A New Dawn Breaks: From Insignificance to Courage
1. Huldah Buntain, *Treasures in Heaven* (New Kingston, PA: Whitaker House, 1989).
2. Calcutta Mercy Hospital website, http://www.calcuttamercyhospital.org/about.
3. Dustin Hedrick, "1949 Revival in the Hebrides Islands, Scotland," *Renaissance of a Soul* (blog) http://holyworldwide.com/dustinhedrick/?p=768.
4. Carolyn Curtis James, *Lost Women of the Bible* (Grand Rapids: Zondervan, 2005), 151.

Chapter 9: Standing on the Rock: From Despair to Faith
1. http://www.garfield.com/comics/vault.html?yr=2008&addr=080728.
2. http://3eanuts.com.
3. http://www.despair.com.
4. Viktor Frankl, *Man's Search for Meaning* (New York: Washington Square Press, 1959).
5. Noah Webster, *American Dictionary of the English Language*, 1828, permission to reprint this edition, G & C Merriam Company, 1967, 1995.
6. Simon Wells, *Power and Passion* (Grand Rapids: Zondervan, 2007), 80.

Chapter 10: On a Clear Day We Can See Home: From Rage to Restoration
1. Tracy Turner, "Alienation leads to school violence, consultant says," *News-Sentinel*, Ft. Wayne, IN, February 21, 2001, http://www.ahaprocess.com/News _Articles/NewsArticle_02212001.html.

About the Author

Sheila Walsh is a powerful communicator, Bible teacher, and best-selling author with more than 4 million books sold. A featured speaker with Women of Faith®, Sheila has reached more than 5 million women by artistically combining honesty, vulnerability, and humor with God's Word.

Author of *God Loves Broken People*, the best-selling memoir *Honestly*, and the Gold Medallion nominee for *The Heartache No One Sees*, Sheila's *The Shelter of God's Promises*, has also been turned into a DVD curriculum and in-depth Bible study. The *Gigi, God's Little Princess* book and video series has won the National Retailer's Choice Award twice and is the most popular Christian brand for young girls in the United States.

Sheila cohosted *The 700 Club* and her own show *Heart to Heart with Sheila Walsh*. She is currently completing her master's in theology.

Twitter @SheilaWalsh, facebook.com/#!sheilawalshconnects

Also Available *from*
SHEILA WALSH

An 8-session Bible study based on *The Storm Inside*

In *The Storm Inside*, an 8-session, video-based Bible study, Sheila unpacks the stories of women from the Bible who faced seemingly insurmountable problems—things like regret, shame, insecurity and heartbreak. And just like the women from the Bible, you can overcome the lies the enemy uses to torment you. You, too, can rely on the truth of God's Word so you can stand during the strongest storms of your life. Designed for use with *The Storm Inside Study Guide*.

Sessions include:

- From Heartbreak to Strength (*Hannah*)
- From Disappointment to Hope (*Woman with Issue of Blood*)
- From Fear to Joy (*Mary Magdalene*)
- From Shame to Love (*Samaritan Woman*)

- From Regret to Rest (*Rahab*)
- From Insecurity, to Confidence (*Ruth*)
- From Insignificance to Courage (*Esther*)
- From Despair to Faith (*Sarah*)

Visit **www.sheilawalsh.com** to learn more.

Available wherever books & Bibles are sold.